Sean M

The Road to God
Knows Where

A Memoir of a Travelling Boyhood

To MAMA

christmas '98

Love from Noel + Mary.

VERITAS

First published 1972 by
The Talbot Press, Dublin

This edition published 1998 by
Veritas Publications
7-8 Lower Abbey Street
Dublin 1

ISBN 1 85390 314 0

British Library Cataloguing
in Publication Data.
A catalogue record for
this book is available
from the British Library.

Cover photograph: ©Fr Browne SJ Collection/
Irish Picture Library. Used with permission.
Cover design by Barbara Croatto
Printed in Ireland by Betaprint Ltd, Dublin

Contents

To Father Tom and many friends so patient and kind;
to 'J' and all the family, and to all on the open road;
this book is dedicated with sincere thanks.

Preface

As an added note to the present edition of *The Road to God Knows Where*, I wish to thank the many great friends whom I have got to know and respect since the book was first published over twenty-five years ago. Many of these great friends have, alas, passed away, but I will always cherish them in my memory. They include Dr Bryan McMahon, Eileen O'Brien, Christy Brown and Eric Cross. Each, in his or her own unique way helped me to love and understand 'the art of the pen'.

I must not forget, however, the great many friends still around after those twenty-five years, still great and wise, both as friends and as mentors: Mathias Oppersdorf and Ed Maher from America; Kevin Etchingham of the Talbot Press days; family friends, especially John and Mag, Joe and Josephine and their families. My appreciation is especially meaningful at this time, on the threshold of a new millennium.

Sean Maher
Dublin
April 1998

Foreword

Sean Maher is a seanchaí of the ancient Irish tradition. Long ago they held a very honoured position in society for it was they who were charged with the responsibility of handing on to coming generations the history and traditions of their people. In this book Sean Maher hands on to us today the traditions, story and culture of the travellers which are not written elsewhere. In this he does a great service not only to his own people but to all of us, for the travellers have been a part of Irish society for over a thousand years. For many centuries they played an important part in Irish life and were made welcome whenever they passed the way. People were glad to avail of their services in repairing utensils that were not easily replaced. They also enjoyed hearing about their travels and their stories.

As society became wealthier and plastic replaced tin and glass, the travellers became more and more isolated. Today great efforts are being made to welcome them again into society and to allow them to use their talents in new ways. If this is to be successful it is essential that we know something of their culture and traditions so that we may accept them as they are and not try to make them 'one of us'.

Over the last thirty years Sean Maher has played an important part in helping his people live in the dignity which they deserve. This book is yet another milestone on *The Road to God knows Where*.

I wish the book every success.

Monsignor G. Thomas Fehily

1

My parents were out-and-out travellers, as were their parents and grandparents before them. My father, when sober, was a great hand at making a living on the open road, my mother being the expert at begging and fortune-telling. Unlike my father, she never drank in her life, itself a rare thing on the road.

My father was a character, a real hard case, a man who lived for a drink. My mother was, by reputation, a great little woman who devoted her time to rearing her children and trying to put some sense into her husband. But it was like battling against a stone wall, for the marriages of the road, as a rule, were for sorrow and hardship. Too often they were match-made, between strangers, and, as such, a lot of unhappiness was bound to follow. My own parents' marriage was a shot-gun affair.

I was born on 15 January 1932 in the county home, or spike, in the town of Tullamore. At the time we were camping about a mile outside the town, in a place known as Collins' Lane. I came into the world on a bitterly cold, snowy morning.

Of my early years there is nothing to tell. I don't remember them and my mother, for all her stories, never had anything remarkable to say about them. I suppose I lived as most other children of the road. I do, however, remember a day when I was three years old. It was the day of my brother's birth and I remember it because of the stout nurse with the funny cap who came to see Mammy. I remember too how the nurse would not allow me into the wagon to see her.

From then on my memory is only too clear. As a very young lad I had a dislike for the road and yet again a liking for it. Summer I liked, winter I loathed. Most of the bad winters, my parents would abandon the tent or wagon and move into a spike for a few months. In those days there was one in every large town in Ireland.

To get into one of these places my parents had to have a ticket from the Local Relieving Officer, and in certain areas it was impossible to get one. Common lodging-houses were active in the 1930s, particularly in Counties Kilkenny and Tipperary, where anyone down-at-heel could stay for a few mideogs* a night. The one I remember most was in Urlingford, County Kilkenny. The building is still there but it is no longer a lodging-house.

This lodging-house was a comical place, as well as being a bit frightening. When my father knocked on the door the night we went there, an old lady with a shawl round her shoulders answered. She took us in, my father, my mother, my sister Nora, my brother Mickeeny and myself.

Her own little room, just inside the door, was festooned with pots and pans of every description, all gleaming beneath the glow of the paraffin lamp. In one corner of the room there was a large brass bed, with a gaudy patchwork quilt over it. In another corner stood a huge clock that ticked loudly as its pendulum swung to and fro. The rest of the room seemed to be full of old trunks and suit-cases and other odds and ends. Against the wall, under a window, there was a long box-like seat with cushions on it, and, purring contentedly, three or four cats gazing intently at a blazing turf fire.

The old lady then took us into another room at the back of the house. It was a very large room. There were two paraffin oil lamps, with reflecting mirrors, hanging on the walls, their globes badly in need of cleaning.

What struck me most, however, when I stepped into this room, was the crowd of people there before me.

'Come in here be the fire, man,' said one old man, 'and bring them little children in; they must be famished with

---

*Note: Mideogs: shillings. Words in Shelta or Cant occur frequently throughout the text. These are explained on pp. 168-71, and a selection of common phrases may also be found on pp. 166-7.

the cold on this winter's night.' 'Hey, Moll,' he shouted to someone, 'get these people a cup of hot scald. Wait a minute!' he cried. 'Well, glory be to God! If it isn't Mickeen and Bridie Devine. And why did you abandon it, the reason to me tell?'

'Abandon what?' asked my father. 'What are you talking about, Jack-the-Halter, you ould divil you? I thought you and Moll were dead years ago.'

'Divil a dead, you can't kill a bad one,' replied Jack-the-Halter. 'Moll and me have given up the road now, our ould bones aren't able for it anymore. We've being staying at this ould lodger for the past year or so. It's better than any spike for we can still travel around the country near here to earn a few bob. You can't do that at a spike. I still have an ould ass and cart, and Moll and me knock out a handy few bob.'

'Do you still do the halters, Jack?' asked my father.

'Divil a bit,' said Jack, 'I don't be able to get up at two or three in the morning now, to go to the horse fairs. God be with the ould days, though. Be the Jakey! Mickeen, you and I spent many a good day at Kilrush and Ballinasloe. What are you doing now, anyway?'

'Mollying as usual,' said my father, 'but we were getting it a bit rough with this bad weather. It's the children we're worried about. It's too bad of weather for them in a tent.'

'Ah, well,' said Jack, 'get into the fireside now and get a feed of stew. The lot of us muck in with the grub; it's rough and ready but it's good. The lie down isn't much, there's two large rooms upstairs with mattresses and blankets to bed down on the floor. The main thing is it's dry and warm; the ould beor of the cean never spares the turf.'

Having listened to Jack-the-Halter, I became less afraid of the place; in fact I got to like it, strange as it was. Jack got his name because all his life he went from fair to fair selling halters and driving horses.

That night we all got our share from the very large pot of stew, after which my mother put down three old mattresses on the floor for me and my brother and sister.

When I was young, staying at the spikes was fun. The

only thing that was wrong at first was my being separated from my mother at night. In all the spikes there was this segregation of the sexes. Even though I was only four or five I still had to sleep in the men's quarters with my father. During the day, however, I was allowed over to the women's side to be with my mother, so that after a while I was satisfied with the arrangement. I liked the spikes very much during the cold winter nights, for I could sit at the big turf fire with my father and all the old men. For me those were my happiest years, for it was then that I was closest to my father. Night after night in the spike he could hold me on his lap near the blazing fire and sing and tell stories to the other men there. This was sheer heaven .... During the day I became my father's messenger to my mother, for he could not see her any time during their stay at the spike. Whenever I went to the women's quarters I always had a few fags hidden inside my gansey to give my mother. When I came back in the evenings, I always had a bit of tea and sugar for my father as well as some message from her. No matter what spike we went to, the routine was always the same. It was hard to adjust to living indoors after having been on the road.

Living in a small house like settled people was harder still. When we first moved into a house in County Kildare, there were my parents, my sister Nora, little Mickeeny, my baby brother, and myself. The house was strange and forbidding, so much so that we only used two downstairs rooms, one for sleeping, the other for cooking, eating and sitting in. The two rooms upstairs we did not use at all.

My father said he didn't like upstairs at all. In a tiny front garden we kept our cart with our camping things – rigging-pole, wattles and cover – still in it.

Within a short space of time, our little house began to look untidy, with old rags, rabbit skins, scrap and the likes strewn around our front door and garden; it was becoming a regular junk heap. This, no doubt, was an annoyance to the neighbours, who complained very strongly. My father and mother told them in no uncertain terms what they could do with their complaints. This led to deeper bitterness and resentment between my parents and their neighbours, and the longer we stayed there the worse things became. Father had to go out to gather scrap and under such circumstances untidiness was inevitable.

I realise now, many, many years later, that my parents had no option but to leave. It was very depressing living in a house. For my father it was almost impossible to get a job of any kind, and living on a few shillings from the St Vincent de Paul Society was a very meagre existence; but this was the only available help for poor people.

Back on the road, I began to re-learn the art of making a living from it. The tinsmith's trade was dead, so that new means of making a living had to be found. My parents tried their hand at everything possible. We, in turn and season, at every house, fair and meeting, mooched our living. Likewise, we sold halters, readers, *Old Moore's Almanacs*, baskets of swag and rolls of waxie. Throughout the country we collected rabbit skins, porter dreepers, jam-jars, old tugs, horsehair, feathers, copper, brass – anything saleable.

In the spring the trade was good for waxie and delf. Most of the articles we hawked were bought wholesale at the 'Monster House' in Kilkenny. When we had saved enough money we moved to Kilkenny to get new stock.

The waxie was bought in rolls of three or five yards and was sold at a fifty per cent profit. We also bought our delf in Kilkenny, oddments in cups, saucers, mugs, plates, mottoes, holy pictures, rosary beads, clay pipes, clothes-pegs, scissors, needles and thread and safety pins. Waxie and delf we bartered as well as sold; we would exchange them for copper, brass, lead, etc.

In the summer we travelled to the 'Meetings': football matches, race meetings, sports, patterns and fairs. At football matches we sold colours, and also ballad sheets, which we used to get by post from a publisher in Cahirciveen. At race-meetings we sold programmes or race-cards, at patterns we sold religious articles and at fairs we sold halters. Along with all this, we begged as well.

In the autumn and winter we concentrated on delf, *Old Moore's Almanacs*, mottoes, Christmas candles and holly decorations.

On the road, every so often, jewmen (as the buyers were known to travellers) would come around in a lorry and buy what feathers, skins, horsehair and scrap we had. There were a lot of these buyers in Ireland at that time.

We attended, at one time or another, almost every big fair or meeting in the twenty-six counties, as did most travellers on the road. We never crossed into Ulster, indeed 95 per cent of the travellers never went near the border at all. My parents used to say, 'That is a very bad part of the country for us poor travellers, too many "Joes", and "Black Joes" at that. The "Joes" down here are all right but them up there are no good.' So we never travelled to Ulster. There are, of course, travellers in those parts, but they have been there for years and very often make excursions down south, but the southern travellers keep well away from Ulster. This fear of Ulster may stem from the customs check when crossing the border. Travellers don't like any stranger going through their belongings.

Football matches were always very good in the summer time, for at these I would sing in the gat ceans and sell colours. The colours were home-made. My mother would buy rolls of ribbons, about an inch wide, nearly always in two colours. She and my father, on the night before the match, would cut the rolls into strips of about an inch long and pin the two different colours together, to be put on the lapel of the football follower's coat for six or nine old pennies.

At a big match, as a mere lad, I often sold three hundred of these colours in a day, and at ninepence each that was no mean living. I was a very persuasive seller as a boy; if a person had a colour I would beg him or her for a penny anyway, so I had the best of both worlds, begging and selling.

My mother too had her own little sideline at these meetings, and that was durriging. She was great at that. She would read hands, the cards, teacups, and even the crystal. What was more important, however, was her unique approach to people whose fortune she wanted to tell. She might be begging or buying something in a shop and she would remark to some lady, or even gent, 'You have a very interesting face ma'am. I can see by your eyes that you have had a bit of sad trouble recently.'

Straight away the person would become interested. As soon as they did my mother would begin: 'Well, ma'am, if you cross your palm with a piece of silver I may able to enlighten you, for I can see joy coming your way.'

This whetted the customer's appetite, so she would give my mother a half-crown piece to cross her hand with. My mother would then proceed with reading the customer's hand, which would be a very brief affair. Nine times out of ten, however, the customer would want – and even ask – to know more; then my mother would say, 'Well ma'am, I have read all there is in your hand, but from it I can see a lot in store for you. To see more, however, I would need to read the cards, or best of all the crystal. To do so, however, it would need a lot of hansel money and as you know hansel money is luck-money. To read the cards would be two pounds but to read the crystal would be five.'

'I could, if you want, ma'am, read a shortened version of the cards, teacup and crystal for seven pounds, the luck number, or I could read the detailed version for three sevens – the three sevens making the luck number of twenty-one. I should warn you, however, that for the luck number of twenty-one I would have to tell you of any sorrows that may have to come your way, but of such I would give you ample warning.'

Now the strange thing about my mother's sideline of fortune-telling was the reaction of her customers. I was with her on hundreds of occasions when she told fortunes, and even though I was only a boy I was always fascinated by the way she told them. What used to strike me more, however, was the reaction of the customers; they were always amazed at how much my mother knew. She always told them the truth. After she had read their fortunes they always told my mother that she was remarkable and very accurate.

I remember asking my mother many times if her fortune-telling was really true.

'Of course not, son,' she would say, 'I just tell them what comes into my head, nothing more. Of course a lot of them tell me that what I say is true, but I don't pay no heed to this. Even when I go back to some of these people years later they ask me to tell their fortune again, as what I told them before had been really true. But again, child, I don't pay much bother to this.'

'Mammy,' I often asked, 'why is it you won't read our fortunes, I mean mine?'

'Why should I, child?' she would reply, 'Sure don't we know our fortune, son, as well as misfortune? I'll tell you one thing, though, when you get big I will tell you your fortune.'

I was never to forget that in fact she did, many years later, tell me my fortune, a fortune that was to become more than true.

My mother was like that. She was a quiet woman throughout her life; whenever she gave advice one could not but see great sense in it, for she was a very great and influencing woman. Her one concern in life was her children. She went through great hardship and suffering for us, as do nearly all poor mothers on the road.

Of course I was also being influenced by the many other people on the tober, but most of all by the stories I heard on our travels, when we went to such great patterns as those at Athenry in County Galway, at Clonmacnoise, Knock, Croagh Patrick and Lough Derg. Great indeed were our meetings with other travellers. The same can be said for the fairs, such as Kilrush, Ballinasloe, Tinahely, Killorglin and many more. Then there were the race meetings at Galway, Tramore, Fairyhouse, Punchestown, Shillelagh and Limerick Junction. Always there was a place and event at which one could meet old friends and new; to swap and trick with, to hear the news about other travellers; to chant at the molly glimmer after the lush. Of course there was the odd row and fight, mostly brought about by differences of opinion over one's daughter's or son's wedding.

Weddings were always a ticklish problem for travellers, especially for the ones to be wed. They, as a rule, had no say in the matter, as their match all too often had been made in some gat-cean over a few dreepers of traipe. On the wedding day, however, the rows were forgotten and all were friends again, as if nothing had ever happened. We were strange people, with strange customs, but always loyal to each other. No outsider ever meant anything to us. Outsiders, or buffers, could never be trusted; they could never have the same loyalty to each other as the travellers.

By the time I was eight I was an expert at making a living on the tober. Although only a child I was as completely aware of the world around me as were my parents. The road life does this to children; it makes them much more self-sufficient than settled children. This in itself is no bad trait, but it can become so when one has to break with the road suddenly.

At the age of eight I was a lad with a great deal of imagination and, believe it or not, a good amount of ambition. The first person to fire my imagination was old Hannora Bell, a distant relation of my mother. But before I tell of our meeting with the Bell family, I must first mention the travellers' need to be with each other. As I said briefly before, we lived in a house for a very short period when I was young, but my parents could not adapt to settled life. In the town where we lived we were not wanted; there was always a great deal of prejudice among the townspeople, especially those who lived near us. For my father it was not too bad because he went out the country each day with the pony and cart. For my mother, however, things were different. She was always alone in the house; none of the neighbours would even talk to her, let alone come into our house for a visit or a cup of tea. To the townspeople we were dirty, begging tinkers and no respectable person would visit us.

When my parents had no option but to go back on the road, my mother was a bit sad. She had begun to like the little house. She knew that living in the house was very lonely, but she wasn't too happy with the thought of going back on the road either, for she knew that, at times, the road could be very lonely too, especially when my father went back on his drinking. However, when he had promised to take the pledge, she said that she would go back on the road with him.

I too had come to like our little house in Mulatty, so much so that I cried on the day my father shut the door of the house for good. My crying made my parents annoyed with me; it also caused an argument between them.

Mother wasn't at all happy with going back on the road, and still longed to settle down. She knew, however, that at the present time settling down was out of question.

When we got a few miles outside the town, my mother said to my father – when I had stopped whinging, of course – 'Mickeen, we seem to be getting bad luck these days. Everything seems to turn against us.'

'Ah, what matter,' he answered. 'It's just as well we left that town, I got sick of the place. We had nowhere to keep the old pony even. As well as this, I have done the country around the town day in and day out. They're getting tired of seeing my face. It won't do any harm to get to a place where our faces will be fresh.'

'I suppose you're right,' said my mother, 'but just the same, there are very lean times everywhere nowadays.'

'Lean or not,' said my father, 'living in that town back there was sheer starvation and any road is better than that. No matter how bad the road is, at least you won't starve on it. How many miserable nights did we sit in that miserable house without a fire, let alone food? No, Bridie, I'm finished with the house for now.'

On occasions like these my parents argued very hotly with each other. My father, of course, felt it very deeply, living in a town and not being able to get a day's work. Living on a few measly shillings' relief was no joke. When he came back from a day's journey around the countryside, having perhaps covered as much as forty miles, he was often depressed, for he was able to collect very little except a few bottles or jam-jars.

The long journeys every day weren't too good for the pony either. During the winter months he got very thin through lack of decent feeding. My father could only take him to graze by the roadside and this always had to be restricted or else he would be fined for the pony's wandering around the roads.

My father and mother had many quarrels in the house, for it could not be otherwise. This led to a great deal of unhappiness. On the road too there is a deal of frustration, but at least there isn't the terrible feeling of being imprisoned as well. And, to such as my parents, this was the awful truth of the whole matter.

For them, living in Mulatty was comparable to existing in complete isolation, and was made more unbearable by the difficult times. It was only natural, therefore, that there should be arguments and quarrels between them. To us children, however, it was puzzling, for we could not understand. These arguments aggravated things between my parents and caused further and deeper problems for everyone, especially the children. I always felt distressed when my parents started to fight with each other. Such, however, is the make-up of the travelling people, and we, the children, have to accept this as life. Seeing this when one is young, during the formative and dangerous years of one's life, does no real good; in fact, more often than not it destroys.

In the end the child can only continue as his parents did before him. For the travellers this is a trait or heritage that has come down through the centuries unchanged by the modern age. Travellers are not able to mix with ordinary society; they can only mix and be happy with their own kind.

I often asked my own mother why she and Dad kept on fighting with each other. 'Ah, don't take no notice of this, alannah,' she would say, 'sure every man and wife has rows. Most of the times it's the drink that causes your Dad to lose his head.'

'Yes, Mammy, I'll say that's right,' I would reply, 'but why is it that people living in houses don't fight with each other all the time?'

'Listen, son,' she would say, 'buffers live their life and we poor travellers live our own; how they live is no concern of ours. I'll tell you one thing though, we travellers never get mixed up in wars and that; buffers do. I know we have fights between ourselves but next day we are as great as ever and even more loyal to each other, and anyway a punch now and then does us no harm. After all, I have given you many a wallop, but you still like me, don't you?'

'Yes, Mammy,' I would reply, 'but this is different.'

'Divil a difference, son', she would say.

'Why are we so different from the buffers?' I would ask.

'It's hard to say, son,' she answered, 'but us poor travellers have been on the road for years and years and years, as long as I can remember, and my parents, God rest them, never wanted to be like the buffers. We were always proud to be travellers and always will be.'

It is only natural for there to be great friction between man and wife on the road. Most of this is caused by heavy drinking. I have seen many rows, leading to fights between travelling families. I have seen a drunk husband, time and time again, battering his wife until she was black and blue. I have seen large family rows stemming from these man-and-wife affairs. Factions on the wife's side and on the husband's would battle with each other – men fighting men, women fighting women, and children fighting children, until there was complete chaos. God help any strangers who should try to stop such a row, especially if they were police. Nine times out of ten the families would stop fighting with each other and vent their wrath on the intruders instead.

The travellers have a strict code with regard to these fights. They see it as their own business to be settled by themselves.

My parents were no better or no worse than any other travelling couple. No matter how hard they might fight, all was soon forgotten and nothing in the world could alter their way of life.

The best row I have ever seen – or should I say *worst* – happened the time we were travelling with Hulla-Hulla Laffan and his wife Maggie, a very simple pair from the Donegal area. Hulla-Hulla got his name because of his dog. He had five greyhounds and every morning he and his hounds would go running through the fields. He kept shouting to the hounds, 'Hulla, hulla! Dogs, go get them rabbits, hulla, hulla.' Thus the name stuck. They had three children, Nellie, May and Eily. The first few days they camped with us were hilarious, and Maggie was the cause. Whilst she was out in the country mooching with my mother one day, she saw a huge heap of sugar beet by the roadside. 'Bridie, woman', she shouted, 'look at yon heap of parsnips.' My mother looked at the beet and started to laugh, but she did not let on why she was laughing. Instead, she decided to go along with Maggie and let her carry on just for the fun of it. 'You'd need a bag to carry them home, Maggie,' she said, 'but maybe we can manage a few between us.'

'Few my eye,' said Maggie, 'I'm going to fill my apron with yon parsnips; 'tisn't every day you'd see great parsnips like yon, and our Hulla-Hulla loves them with a pig's head and cabbage.'

Maggie went to the heap of sugar beet and loaded her apron with twelve or so of the largest she could find. My mother, to keep up the joke, put some in her apron also.

When my mother got home she told my father all about Maggie and the beet. 'Well don't say anything,' said father. 'We'll see what happens.'

That night Maggie peeled and cut the beet and put it in a large pot with potatoes, cabbage and half a pig's head. An hour or so later we could hear shouting on at the other camp between Hulla Hulla and Maggie. The next minute Maggie came tearing down the road to our camp, crying.

'What's wrong, Maggie?' asked my mother.

'Yon feen of mine, Bridie,' she said, 'he's never satisfied, he's worse than them hounds of his.'

'What do you mean, Maggie?' asked my mother.

'What do I mean?' asked Maggie, 'I don't really know. Yon man of mine said I pickled the dinner with sugar and I think he's going a bit barmy. You know, Bridie, I spent over five hours boiling that supper over one of the best fires you ever seen. The spuds, meat and cabbage boiled quickly but yon parsnips were a divil to cook. After all this I get nothing but abuse; sugar indeed! He's imagining things.'

'Did you taste the dinner, Maggie?' asked my father.

'I didn't get the time, Mickeen. I was just getting a bit ready for the children when the husband ups and knocks me flying with a punch.'

As she was saying this, Hulla-Hulla came tearing down the road shouting, 'Come up here you red-headed witch and get me some supper. Don't mind you prating there with the Devines, they're only making a laughing-stock of you.'

'What are you saying, you dirty-looking hound you?' roared Maggie. 'You're no better than them hounds of yours! Well, to hell with you and your hounds, you can get someone else to cook for you.'

At that, Hulla Hulla caught hold of his wife by the hair with one hand and punched her repeatedly in the face with the other; at the same time he dragged her along the road back towards their own camp. Maggie was screaming in pain. For about ten minutes the screaming went on, as also did the roars of their frightened children. Suddenly there was quiet.

The next morning the row was forgotten, but Maggie's face was battered and scarred and swollen, so much so that she had to remain in bed for about a week after. My parents were powerless to help, for it was a row between man and wife, and on the road such rows must never be interfered with. There is cruelty on the road, but then again there is great love and kindredship among travellers that overcomes all hardships.

2

The year is 1939 and I am just seven years old. It has been a year now since I left Mulatty with my parents and brother and sister, a year of travelling the road and sleeping in the tent. I have not forgotten Mulatty and the many little friends there and yearn for the place a little. I remember with deep resentment the punch I got from my father that day we left our little house. I cried because I didn't want to leave and he punched me, I feel now, because he really didn't want to leave either. Being veteran travellers, my parents knew full well the hardship of the road and the great loneliness that is part and parcel of it. You only have to leave the bustle of a town behind you for the shelter of a wet ditch on a by-road to know what loneliness is. But a punch didn't cure my loneliness, nor my parents' either.

'Mickeen,' my mother asked one night at the fire, some time later, 'do you know who I was talking to today in Templemore?'

'No,' said my father, 'who?'

'Hannora Bell and her mother Lizzie.'

'Was old Jack Bell with them?'

'No,' said my mother, 'he was out at the camp minding their son Tommy's two children.'

'Bedad, it's years since I saw Jack. Did Lizzie say where they were camping?'

'Yes,' she said, 'they're camping about a mile out on the Thurles Road. She asked me to pull out there with them, if we were going to stay around these parts. So I told her that you might do so tomorrow.'

'Bedad we will go out then, Bridie. It'll be a bit of company for us.'

'How is Hannora these days? Did she find a husband yet?' asked my father.

'No, she's still the same Hannora, humming her words as usual.'

The following day we moved out to where the Bell family were camped. We stayed travelling around with them for six months or so. We all had a lot to talk about and over a roaring fire of sticks at night many stories and episodes of the good old days were related.

The Bell family were very simple people. There was old Jack and his wife Lizzie, who were in their late seventies. They had two children, one of whom, Tommy, was now twenty-eight years of age and married to Peg. They had two children, both boys, whose ages were eight and ten. They were known mostly by their nicknames, as Twister and Spike, Twister being the older boy. Then there was Hannora, Jack and Lizzie's daughter, a woman of fifty-two or so and still a spinster. Hannora and Tommy were a bit simple in their ways and had been so from their earliest years. Living with the Bell family was always a pleasure, for there was no end to the amusement they, in their simple ways and quite unintentionally, of course, gave to those who travelled with them.

I was delighted to travel with the Bell family, having become firm friends with Twister. Something else was happening too; I had, within a few weeks, become very attached to Hannora and she to me. This came about when she asked my mother if she could take me with her to mooch the town. Having a gallia was a good excuse for mooching for travellers. My mother agreed.

'You can take him any time, Hannora, but he'll make a bad moocher.'

'Oh I don't mind that, Bridie,' said Hannora, 'it'll be a bit of company for me anyway. I can't take them yokes of Tommy's because they are pure wild and play me up something terrible.'

'You'll not have to worry about that with Sean. At times he is too quiet when I take him out,' said my mother.

'Hi, Sean!' Hannora shouted when she caught sight of me playing on the road, 'come'ere a minute will you, son?'

'What do you want, Hannora?' I said.

'Do you want to come in to mooch the town with me today?'

'Is Twister coming too?' I asked.

'No, he can't come today because he's going out in the cart with his father,' replied Hannora.

'All right then, I'll go. Are we going now?'

'Yes, as soon as I rack me old hair, we'll be off in the name of God,' said Hannora.

My mother gave me a cow's lick with a piece of wet cloth and combed my matted black hair as best as she could. When all was done, Hannora and I headed on foot to mooch Templemore, because the soldiers were stationed there and Wednesday was their pay day.

I liked Hannora, especially when she talked, because she had a habit of humming after each sentence she spoke.

'Hannora.'

'Yes?'

'Why do you hum when you talk? You always say hmm.'

'Oh I do that so that I will get more grade when I mooch hmm. The people take more pity on me, hmm.'

'But you are not mooching now and still you hmm.'

'I does that so that I learns the habit better, alannah, hmm,' said Hannora. 'Why does it bother you, anyway?'

'It's funny, that's why,' I replied.

'Yeah, well you should not pass remarks.'

'No, I'm not passing remarks, I like you 'cause you do that,' I replied.

'Oh, in that case it's all right, only some people makes fun of me 'cause I do that, especially young ones,' said Hannora.

'I don't ever make fun of you, Hannora,' said I seriously, 'and you know that.'

'Yes I know, 'cause if you did I would not take you with me,' said Hannora.

'Do you like me, Hannora?' I asked suddenly.

'Yes, of course I do, whatever brought that into your little nopper?'

'Nothing,' I answered, 'but I like you a lot.'

'Look Seáneen,' said Hannora, 'can you mooch? That's what I'd like to know!'

'Of course I can mooch, Mammy said I'm a topping little moocher.'

'She did, did she,' said Hannora, 'well that's good enough for me.'

'Hannora?' I asked.

'Yes, Seáneen.'

'How long have you been smoking the clay pipe?'

'I declare to goodness,' said Hannora, taking the little clay pipe that she was smoking from her mouth and spitting on the road, 'you do ask some funny questions. Anyway I've been smoking the pipe for years.'

'Even when you were small?' I asked.

'Even when I was small,' replied Hannora.

'Even when you were as small as me?'

'Even when I was as small as you, hmm,' replied Hannora.

'Hannora, can I smoke a pipe?' I asked.

'But child, you are too small and it would stop you growing.'

'Hannora, if you let me have a smoke of the pipe I will mooch real well.'

'Listen, child, I could not let you smoke, because your mother would kill me; the pipe smoking would make you sick,' said Hannora.

I did not give in easily, I kept on asking Hannora throughout the day about the pipe. She was very pleased with herself for having taken me with her, for she found that I was quite a good little moocher. I was especially so in the pubs, where I nipped in and out unnoticed by the bar-staff. Altogether, I picked up quite a few shillings tapping the wobs in the pubs. Hannora herself was good at mooching. She always wore a big black shawl. Inside it she had a few old coats wrapped up to resemble a baby, which is always a great help.

We left town at about seven and headed home. On the

way she finally gave in to my entreaties for a smoke of the pipe. She lit it and gave it to me. Straight away I began smoking, between coughs and spits, and kept it up for about ten minutes. Hannora had a terrible time trying to get the pipe back.

She was hoping that I would not get sick, but her hope was in vain. Soon I became as white as a sheet and poor Hannora became terribly worried now.

'I told you, didn't I?' she said. 'But no, you wouldn't listen, would you?'

'I feel terrible, Hannora, am I going to die?' I asked, and began crying a little.

'No, child, of course you're not going to die, you are just a little sick and it'll go away in a minute. All you have to do is sit down for a few minutes,' said Hannora. 'Come on now, sit down on the grass there and you'll be all right.'

I proceeded to vomit all over the place, which was a great relief. I sat down for about ten minutes, after which I felt better.

'Come on now, Hannora,' I said.

'Good boy, come on, then, I bet you'll never smoke a pipe again.'

'Begosh I won't,' I said, 'they make me stomach feel terrible bad.'

'I told you so, but you wouldn't believe me, would you?'

'I do now though, don't I?'

'You do indeed, alannah, God bless you, hmm.'

'Hannora, did we mooch much grade today in the helm?'

'Well son, we did very well today, thanks be to God,' she replied. 'As you can see, me ould mangie is full. Besides this, the ould grade sack is hefty too. You know, alannah, you'll be a right feen for some lucky beor when you grow up, please God, for you are a topping little knocker-out. Musha, I wish I were a strip of a laceen again.'

'I'll be like you, Hannora,' I said, 'because I'll never get married. Instead I'll be a cunic or something.'

'A cunic!' cried Hannora, 'that's a good one. Still, it mightn't be too bad at that.'

'Why is it that you never married, Hannora?' I asked her.

'Well,' replied Hannora with surprise, 'I wasn't satisfied with the object that was picked to marry me. To make things worse he wasn't even a whole idiot, he was only a half idiot, if you see what I mean like.'

'Who picked him for you?' I asked.

'Oh, my parents did,' said Hannora. 'Sure they were worse fools anyway, but they will believe in this matchmaking thing.'

'Matchmaking!' I said. 'What's matchmaking, Hannora?'

'Well, son, it's a way that travellers have of getting a husband or wife for their son or daughter, as the case may be,' replied Hannora.

'Well, why didn't you pick your own husband, Hannora?'

'Why indeed, son! Well it's not as easy as that; besides, it's a long story and I'm sure you wouldn't be interested in the likes of that at your age,' answered Hannora.

'Oh I would, Hannora,' I pleaded, 'honestly I would, I swear it!'

'Well, matchmaking is a very old custom with the travellers in Ireland. The reason for matchmaking is to ensure that a pavvy beor marries a pavvy fean and not a buffer.

'Now when a sublia and laceen on the tober come to courting age, they are thought of as being in danger. You see a girl or boy might fall in love with the first one they meet. If it wasn't for the buffers there would be no problem; but the one great fear of the pavvies is that their children might fall in love with heartless buffers and, make no mistake, to the travellers all outsiders are heartless people. It is known that when a pavvy marries a buffer they are made to lead a comeragh's life.

'This, alannah,' she continued, 'is why the pavvies have matchmaking. Matchmaking has been a custom with us since early Christian times and even before this. In truth, alannah, matchmaking was first introduced in Ireland by the pavvies.

'Of course the buffers here in Ireland have their matchmaking but this is done for money or personal gain and not for the protection and happiness of the people for whom they matchmake. This is a vast difference between matchmaking by the buffers and the pavvies.

'Nowadays,' continued Hannora, 'there isn't much need for matchmaking as such, but, God help us, the poor travellers are still very much afraid of their children getting married to outsiders, to be taken away to some foreign land and treated as slaves.

'All in all, Seáneen,' she continued, 'more can be prated in favour of matchmaking than against, in a sense. Even myself, ould grey-headed crone that I am, agree with matchmaking, but I would never hold with a match that was made between two young pavvies that are meeting for the first time. I would never agree with this because I believe, after all, that this too often is a marriage of convenience and a loveless marriage as well. It was such with me, when I was a slip of a girl. A match was made in a pub in Bansha for me and a young pavvy called Humpy Joe.

'I can tell you, alannah,' continued Hannora, 'that when I took one gawk at the feen with the larry on his back I soon took to my heels through the sarks. I wasn't seen for days after, but when I was eventually found, my father still wanted me to marry the Hump.

'Well, love, I got beaten about ten times, but I still wouldn't give in. Me father was wild and said that I would disgrace his name on the road if I did not go through with the match.

'Well, disgrace or no, I made up me mind that, even if I was to be killed stone dead, I would not go through with the marriage.

'My refusal to marry caused a great row between Humpy's father and mine. In fact, the two of them hammered each other on the road near the molly over it. My father ended up getting about ten stitches on his face. But, as is always the case, all was forgiven and forgotten the next day. It was decided that they could wait for another day to renew the wedding match.

'Well, child, as you can see, they are still waiting for poor ould Hannora to marry and I'm afraid that they'll have to wait a lot longer. For on that day I vowed I would never marry, happy in me own ould way, thank God, hmm.'

All through the story I felt for Hannora, and when she had finished I asked in my childish way, 'Hannora, will you marry me when I grow up?'

'Of course I will, child, of course I will. Why else,' she joked, 'do you think I've waited all these years? But hould your hoult a minute, I thought you said that you were never going to marry?'

'Neither I wasn't,' I replied, 'until you told me that story.'

'Ah, I was wondering about this back on the road a bit when I saw the two magpies. I hope though that this omen of joys is not spoiled by some mog of a comeragh coming out on the road to do the cake-walk.'

'What do you mean, Hannora, by cake-walk and magpies?' I asked. 'I didn't see them. Will you tell us about them, Hannora? I love listening to you telling stories, honest to God I do!'

'Well, alannah,' she said, 'we've had a good day, thank God, but we have a tidy bit to walk to get home, so I might as well shorten the journey for you by telling you the story. How about that, Seáneen?'

'I hope it will shorten the road,' I said, 'cause me feet are sore.'

'Hundreds of years ago in Ireland,' said she, 'when there was no such things as cars or engines or even smooth roads like now, the travellers led a particularly lonely life. They had, however, one great friend in the form of a blind story-teller. Where he came from or who he really was is yet a mystery – but more about that later on.

'Anyway,' Hannora continued, 'he was first noticed on a lonely bog road outside the town of Edenderry, and, mind you, this was hundreds of years ago. Anyway, when he was first seen and heard of it was at a roadside wake. A travelling woman and her young children and relatives were mourning the death of her husband who died suddenly.

'The body of the dead husband was laid out on a straw bed in the shelter tent with a goat-grease candle lighted on either side of the corpse, which enhanced the loneliness of the scene for the poor unfortunate mourners.

'Well,' continued Hannora, 'this lonely and sad roadside waking was interrupted by a strange and lovely voice, "My brethren of the road, I am deeply moved by your great sorrow and I would like, if I could at all, to try and lessen the heavy grief of your heart."

'Everyone at the wake that night turned around in awe to see who had spoken. There, before their very eyes, stood a very mysterious, but very appealing old man. He was dressed in a long, flowing white robe, and had equally long white hair, which had a silvery sheen that reflected the light of the goat-grease candles. Most remarkable of all was the serene look on the old man's face and, in particular, his piercing blue eyes. Everyone at the wake that night also noticed that, perched on the old man's right shoulder, was a piebald bird, a magpie.

' "Indeed, sir," said the bereaved widow, "there is little you can do to help me in the loss of my dear husband."

' "True, dear woman," said the old man. "But to one such as I, a stranger to all you humble people, death, birth and marriage – in fact, in all that is sorrow and joy on the road – it has been my lot to share with those who are beset by such."

' "Though I look on this sad scene tonight, I see not your faces, for eyes to see I do not have. Instead my heart feels every ache and pain of such loss as yours, humble broken-hearted mother. For my sight I have here, on my shoulder, the bird of sorrow.

> Of such birds I have seven;
> One for sorrow,
> Two for joy,
> Three for a girl,
> Four for a boy,
> Five for crosses,

Six for losses,
And seven for a secret never told."

'Well,' continued Hannora, 'you can imagine the surprise on everyone's face at that molly on hearing this old stranger talk. Normally they would have run the old feen, thinking that he must be an old ruilla feen, but they did not. Rather, they told the old man to come and sit with them and have some light refreshment. In other words, they took him instantly as if he had been one of their own.

'Then, God bless the mark!' continued Hannora, 'as if from out of thin air, another bird perched on the shoulder of the old man and, as if by magic, not one felt sad but instead everyone became happy.'

' "Ah," said the old man, "the second bird has come, so you will not feel unhappy or sad now; soon three more birds shall come, then your late husband will lie in his final happy rest with a cross to mark the spot."

'Do you know,' continued Hannora, 'that within a very short while the other three magpies appeared and without question all the people at the wake made the grave and buried the dead man. Having done so, they put a little wooden cross over the grave. There was no more sorrow.

'After a while everyone – including the old blind man – sat around a big blazing fire in the shelter tent. After a very happy and enjoyable meal the old man began talking again, without any prompting from his astonished, but eager and happy listeners.

' "In a while now," he said, "two more birds shall come, making the total seven, and seven is for a secret never to be told. I know only too well that you are curious to find out who I am. To find out this, though, you are bound, by the appearance of the seven birds, to reveal the secret to none other than the people of the road.

' "I have been of the road for many, many years, indeed for many, many centuries. Now I am feebled by my great age and blindness; but though I shall soon roam the roads no more, my birds, the magpies, shall continue in my place and all travellers meeting them shall know whether sorrow or joy shall come their way. These birds will be a sign for travellers so that they can remember me and will also warn them in advance of any sorrow or joy.

' "Now," the old man continued, "as you can see, the seven birds are here, so it is time, and you shall be the only family that shall ever know my true identity. Many who follow will try to discover who I was, but only you shall know. One day, however, centuries hence, others will get to know the secret, and then, and only then, will there be happiness in the heart of everyone in Ireland." '

'Well,' said Hannora, 'that's the end of the story, and to this very day no one knows who the old man was. The travellers who met and spoke to him so long ago brought the secret with them to their graves.'

'What a pity,' I said, 'the story was only getting interesting when the seven magpies appeared. I'd love to know who he was.'

'So would I, alannah,' said Hannora, 'but that was a secret and one that has so far remained so.'

'Who do you think he was?'

'I don't know,' said Hannora, 'some people have said it was St Patrick, others said St Kevin, and some have even said it was the travellers' patron, St Christopher. One thing, however, everyone is sure of, is that the man was a saint.'

'Oh, that reminds me, Hannora,' I said, 'you never told me the story about the dog that cake-walks.'

'Oh, you and your stories, Seáneen. All right then, we have still a biteen to walk and it's only a short one, so I'll tell it for what it's worth,' said Hannora. 'Now, I don't know whether you know it or not, but there is one thing that you will very seldom see and that is a dog walking. If you take notice in future you will see that a dog always trots along or gallops but never actually walks, and, God bless the mark, I hope you never do; you won't help but notice for the simple reason that when a dog walks it is a comical sight, for he walks even more comical than a penguin.

'For a person to see a dog doing the cake-walk is disaster.

For it means the break-up of a marriage or a runaway marriage that will end up bad for the person who saw it. The cake-walk gets its name from the wedding cake. So the person who sees a dog doing the cake-walk is destined to experience a cake-walk wedding.

'So you see, alannah,' said Hannora, 'it is a dangerous thing to see a dog doing the cake-walk.'

So it was with Hannora. I became very fond of her and was forever pestering her to tell me stories – which she always did with pleasure. She knew hundreds of stories and had an almost magical way of relating each one, making every word come alive.

Yes indeed, Hannora and I became very fond of each other. Every time she went mooching she brought me with her, and sometimes Twister came too. Whenever he came, however, things got out of hand for poor Hannora, for when us two boys got together there was ructions. We used to get up to all sorts of capers on the road. We would chase the life out of some poor farmer's fowl or do some other such devilment. It was for this reason that Hannora did not bring us both with her so often.

Staying with the Bells was doing me the world of good for I was enjoying every minute of it. I had new friends.

A few weeks after meeting the Bell family we all moved together to Thurles in County Tipperary. And when we got to the well-known camping ground we found we had still more company already there in the form of Jim the Fiddler.

The place was K's Avenue near Thurles. There was Jim, his wife Biddie, and 'Ghosty'. They were living in a 'commodation' – a two-wheeled wagon. The Fiddler and his son used to busk the helms whilst his wife did the knobbing.

My father and mother and the Bell family knew the Fiddlers well; they had another name but they were only called the Fiddlers because of their gift of playing the instruments. But it had been years since they last met. Twister, Spike and I were meeting the Fiddlers for the first time.

As is the custom when travellers meet like this after so long, the elders get into chat straight away about the old times. Then they pass on the various news to each other about other families they may have met on their travels. Us children, however, that's if we were meeting for the first time, would act shy until we got to know each other better.

Within a day I became great pals with Ghosty. In fact when we met up with the Fiddlers, life for us became a pleasure, for they were great company. I remember very well the hooly that was held at the molly that first night we were with them. Jim the Fiddler, my father and Hannora's father went in and busked the town of Thurles; between them they made a right few deener. Then they went and got well traiped, bought a lot more traipe and brought it out to the molly.

Well, there was the finest shindig I have seen for many a year at the molly that night. There was a big roaring stick fire and everyone had a hearty peck of fé, cunnions and salery. To make it even better, we had the finest of grunter's carnish pickled with salan.

After the feed and the drink the night really started. Jim and his son got their diffles and there was song and dance by the roadside until the early hours of the morning. In turn each of us, young and old, would sing a song with the Fiddlers accompanying.

I remember to this day the old songs that were sung that night and have been sung on many a night since. Songs like 'The Lakes of Collfin', 'Tubberara', 'The Ould Plaid Shawl', 'The Golly Pavvy', 'The Murder of a Travelling Lad', and many many more.

The Murder of a Travelling Lad
I am the son of a pavvy-man,
A gosoon of the road.
I've lived as have my parents lived,
And carried me bitter load;
To beg a meal and spoke a wheel
O'er many a hill an' dale,

And oft beneath me dusty heel,
No shoes to keep me warm.

In winter's cold, cold weather,
My clothes were always thin.
Upon me back a mooching sack,
And on me face a grin.
With these I faced the cruel road,
As tears well'd in me eyes;
For broken-hearted son was I,
And doleful were me sighs.

It all began some years ago,
When I was a weeny lad.
Mother died, God rest her soul,
And father took quite bad;
For a man as he, to lose a wife,
Was a man bereft of joy;
And on the road, no word he spoke
Since mother's final sigh.

For three long years I watch'd him fade,
As does the setting sun;
For three long years without a word,
I was a lonely son.
Every day I pray'd to God
That father would get well:
But now he dwells in holy ground,
Near the town of sweet Clonmel.

Now bereft am I of reason,
Behind these gloomy walls:
No more to walk the open roads,
Until me Maker calls.
No more can I, though still a boy,
Seek freedom from my doom;
For here I lie and here I die,
In this lonely darken'd room.

Then murder'd soul, I surely am,
Though life be in me heart.
Me tomb is made of granite stone,
And me keepers play their part;
Night and day they watch o'er me,
And make each day more sad,
And few remember, when they pray,
The murder'd travelling lad.

On such nights the road was heaven for me, for then I would become enraptured by the whole scene. The strong odours of the drink and the smoke from the burning sticks on the fire, the smell of the bacon and cabbage, and this, intermingled with the scents of the country night, of new cut grass, of nearby cattle and the many other scents, gave a very strange picture and a feeling of happiness and contentment.

I suppose it may seem odd, but today these are the things I miss, these are the things I long to experience again.

The travellers' gift of singing old folk songs is uncanny. Some of their songs are ages old and have been passed down through the centuries from father to son. Most of all, when a traveller sings a song he puts great feeling into every word, just like someone narrating a tale. You are able to feel the action of the song, as if it were happening as the song is being sung. Whether it was a lament, dirge or jollification, the feeling was always real. The travellers have a host of songs praising or lamenting their fellow brethren, long since dead. These are in the form of a life-story in verse.

They have, however, one other great gift – that of story-telling. They are born story-tellers. Their stories and legends are legion. Some of them reach very far back in history and are passed down through the years by word of mouth, from father to son. In these stories one hears of famous European legends, but most of all those of travellers who were famous many many ages ago.

The greatest listeners to these tales and legends are, of course, the travelling children. They will sit enraptured for hours and hours, without making a sound. This is their world, listening to stories, and their one means of education. It is indeed a wonderful experience to look at a crowd of travellers on a dark night, men, women and children sitting around an open, roaring fire, listening to one of their number narrating a story.

I loved, above all else, hearing stories. At night, I would relive in my dreams the tales I heard. I liked especially the many, many ghost stories I heard; stories about the banshee, the dead-coach with its headless driver, stories of haunted houses and by-ways and the like. The whole thing about this gift for story-telling lies in the way the narrator tells it. He can create an uncannily realistic atmosphere when telling a story.

Of course, story-time only came when the elder travellers were sober. When they were drunk, a sing-song took the place of stories, or else a good row and fight with each other. Happily, however, this was not a regular thing.

We remained around Thurles for about four months with the Bell family and the Fiddler family. I spent most of this time with Ghosty and Twister. Sometimes the three of us would go together into the town and mooch the pubs. Ghosty would play the fiddle whilst Twister and I would sing. We used to do well together, often picking up three or four pounds for a few hours of work. At the end we would have a share-out with the money and then go out to the cinema, but always making sure to save some of the money we earned to bring home. At the cinema we would spend only a few shillings each.

'Ghosty,' I asked one day, 'how did you get your name?'

'Because,' he said, 'I was supposed to have been born on or in some haunted lane – Collins' Lane it's called; someone was drowned there who is supposed to have been seen several times since.'

'I don't believe you,' said Twister, 'you made that up.'

'I swear, as true as I'm here, I didn't make it up. You can ask me daddy if you don't believe me, honestly,' he said.

'I believe you, Ghosty, but tell us, how do you know that

the road is really haunted?' I asked. 'After all, your mammy and daddy might've been codding you, for all you know.'

'No, they don't cod like that; besides, other people have seen the ghost in this lane.'

'Well, tell us then, how he is supposed to be seen?' I asked, dying to hear the full story.

'Okay,' said Ghosty, 'come on and sit down and I will tell ye if you want to hear, but me daddy could tell it better and if you like I will ask him to tell it to everyone tonight like he's done before.'

Sure enough, that night, when everyone was seated round the fire, the Fiddler told the story of how his son got his name. During the telling of the story one could hear a pin drop on the grass. Save for the very odd hoot of an owl or the distant bark of a vixen, it was deadly silent.

'Well,' began the Fiddler, 'as sure as I am sitting on this roadside tonight, the following story is the honest truth. It all began on a late summer's night when we pulled into this little lane. My wife was not too well – she was expecting Ghosty at the time – so I pulled into the lane and made the camp as fast as I could. I wanted to get the wife into bed so she could rest.

'Anyway,' he continued, 'I got the camp down and the wife went in and lay down. In the meantime I rummaged through the hedge beside us to get a lock of sticks to make a fire with and make a dropeen of tea. We had plenty of chuck and we were very crolish.

'I made the tea and fried a bit of bacon and a few eggs and we ate them between us. After this the wife lay down again. The door of the tent was open and I could see her plainly in the firelight.

' "Are you feeling better now?" I asked her. She said that she was. She then asked me if I was going to bed and I told her I would do when I had had a smoke.

'Anyway, I sat by the fire with my back to the hedge smoking a fag on my own. It was a good night and the sky was clear so I sat up a bit longer. I wasn't feeling tired, but I was worried about the wife being unwell and I really waited up so that she could drop off to sleep.

'About half an hour or so later – it must have been nearly one in the morning – my wife called up and whispered, "Jim, what does that sham want?"

' "What sham?" I said, looking up from my intent gazing at the fire.

' "The sham standing on the tober in front of you."

'At first I did not see anyone, because I could not get accustomed to the darkness beyond the fire. Then, God bless us and save us here this night, I saw the man standing on the road in front of the fire staring at me. I got a bit of a start at first because, I thought, how on earth was it that I did not hear his footsteps as he approached? "Goodnight, sir," I said to him, but no answer. "It's a grand night, God bless it," I said, but still no answer. I then stood up and walked towards him, thinking that he might be lushed.

'Then, God bless the mark, I saw his face; it was covered with blood and very badly scarred. But the thing that gave me the fright was the broad smile on his face. First I felt myself feel faint, then cold sweat covered my whole body. I became glued to the ground, still staring at the face of the stranger a few feet in front of me. Hard as I tried I could not move; I tried to speak but couldn't. My mouth seemed locked. I must have been there only a few minutes but it seemed a lifetime then.

'Then, without the slightest warning, the man disappeared before my very eyes. "Is he gone?" my wife asked, poking her head out of the door of the tent.

'"Gone," I said, "is putting it mildly; in reality he has vanished, whoever he was, and he looks like he's had a terrible hiding or was in some kind of car crash. Whatever it was, he could not talk anyway."

' "Maybe the poor chap's suffering from shock or something," said my wife. "Do you think we should tell someone about it?"

'"Not me, anyhow," said I, "there is something very strange about that man. Do you know that I got the fright of my life? I was speechless and felt very funny the moment I saw him. No, whoever he was, he'll have to wait until morning."

'With that,' the Fiddler said, 'we retired for the night, but it was a night that I shall never forget, God save us from harm. At about three o'clock that same morning my wife and I were again awakened. "Jim," said my wife, "that's a curra trotting or galloping down the road. Look out," she said, "and see who it is." I looked out, and then got my second shock that night, God bless and save us, for, galloping down the road like mad was my own old grey pony. "It's Dolly," I told my wife, "there must be some blackguard running her away from the camp." With that I jumped out of bed, put on my trousers, and ran in my bare feet down the road after Dolly. I had only gone a few yards when she came galloping back towards the camp again. I stepped out in the middle of the road, with my hands stretched out sideways to try and stop the pony. Then Dolly came like a demon snorting like hell. She did not even slow down when she got near me; I had to jump out of the way because she was bearing right down on me. As I got out of the way, Dolly sailed by at full speed, still snorting. I looked to see if anyone was following her but the road was deserted. That's strange, I said myself, but maybe whoever was chasing Dolly had seen me and had scooted.

'I came back towards the camp again and as I reached it Dolly came back down the road again in full gallop and still snorting. By now, as you can imagine,' the Fiddler continued, 'I was a very worried man. I began to think that Dolly must be suffering from fits or something – you know, like a dog gets. I knew there was nothing I could do on my own. As well as this, I was twice as worried about the wife now. The pony's strange behaviour would be bound to worry and frighten her.

'I went into the tent, and the wife was indeed feeling bad. She told me she was in pain, so I said I would go for a doctor. She told me she would be all right, but I was to hurry. So off I ran to the town which was about a mile or so away. In my worry over the wife I forgot the pony and everything else; as I ran I prayed that my wife would be well and that nothing would happen to her this awful night.

'When I got to the town I went straight to the garda station and told the garda on duty about my wife's sudden illness. He rang up the local doctor. In about ten minutes I was heading out for the camp with the doctor and a nurse in the doctor's car. About an hour after arriving at the camp my wife gave birth to our first child, which was Ghosty here. After the birth my wife and the baby were taken to the hospital where they remained for a week or so.

'By the time they left for the hospital it was seven a.m. and the sun was beginning to shine. I was exhausted, so I lay down for an hour or so. When I awoke I took stock of the place where I was camping. Everything looked normal so I began a search for Dolly. I must have walked about two miles or so but came back to the camp again because I was completely tired; what with the night's carry-on and the missing pony, I just could not take any more. I decided to make a drop of tea. I went in to the old field by the side of the camp to get a lock of sticks to make a fire. As I was rooting along the hedge I came to an old quarry. I went to the edge and looked in, through curiosity, only to stop in my tracks with shock and disbelief.

'Well, everyone, you'd never believe what I saw lying at the bottom of that old quarry that dreadful morning, the morning of my son's birth too. Well, let me tell you, it was Dolly; yes, the pony was lying dead in that old quarry. Whoever was driving Dolly during the night had driven her off the edge to be killed on the rocks down below. I stood there, numbed with shock, gazing down at the old pony. "God," I said, when I could open my lips again, "how could anyone be so cruel as to drive that poor animal to such a horrible end?" A poor old beast that had taken me and the wife through the best part of Ireland in the couple of years we had her.

'As I was standing there, looking down at the dead pony, a man had come across the field to where I was without my noticing him. When he got alongside me, he saw the pony and said, "Is that yours down there?"

' "Yes, yes indeed, sir, it is, or was until someone drove it to death down there."

' "That's funny," said the man, "that's the second horse that was killed in that old quarry within two years. The only difference is that the last one had a young rider on its back, and both rider and horse were killed, Lord have mercy on the poor chap. He was only a young fellow of nineteen or twenty. It was a terrible tragedy for his poor parents. He was a travelling chap too. There," the man pointed, "is the little wooden cross his family put up in his memory."

' "Your pony must've stumbled in there in the dark," the man continued, "I always said they should put a big fence all around this old quarry."

'Well, you can imagine what my thoughts were on hearing this from the man. I did not, of course, tell him about what happened the night before. I never said a word about the man with the cut face or about the pony running up and down the road, but I did ask him if the chap who was killed had been badly cut. He told me that his face was smashed in on the rocks. I then asked the man what could I do about the dead pony.

' "You leave that to me," he said, "I will get some people out here with a lorry who will only too gladly cart it away. How are you going to manage?" he asked then.

' "Oh, I'll move straight away so that I can get nearer to the town."

' "But how will you manage the cart without a pony?"

' "Oh that'll be easy," I said, "I'll pull it myself as far as the town; in a week or two I may be able to get another pony, or even a donkey."

' "I'll tell you what, then," said the man, "you pack up all your things and I'll go up and bring down my pony to pull your cart into the town; I'll come in with you and I'll ride him back out."

' "Thank you very much, sir," I said, "this is very kind of you."

' "Nothing at all," he said, "I'm only too glad to help out."

'I needn't tell you that I packed up camp in double-quick time, to get away from the unlucky place! I was convinced now, beyond all doubt, that the man who appeared with the cut face was the ghost of that unfortunate traveller who was killed. Somehow or other we must have disturbed his rest and the result was the death of the pony.

'The farmer who said the pony must have stumbled in was, of course, quite wrong. Dolly was a pony who would never jump over a hedge to get into a field on her own. She was always used to grazing by the roadside. Indeed, Dolly was a real old pet and would never go very far from the camp at all, winter or summer. No, Dolly was driven to her death and only a spirit of some kind would have made her jump into that quarry.'

The Fiddler had finished his story and we, his enraptured listeners, relaxed and moved in a bubble of talk for the first time since the beginning of the tale. Many of us, the younger listeners, had crouched near to our parents during the narration of the story because we had become scared as it moved along.

'My,' said my dad, 'that was indeed a bad night for you and the wife. But do you know, I heard about this from other travellers a few years ago, but didn't believe them; I thought they were pulling my leg. I know different now. It goes to show that there are some roads and places haunted throughout Ireland. That's why I'm always very careful about where I camp nowadays.'

I was completely carried away by this tale; I kept looking at Ghosty as I tried to visualise the actual happenings of that night. In my mind I felt as if I had actually been there that night, so engrossed had I become in the tale as it was told. I was always very frightened by such tales, but no matter how scared I was I could not resist listening to them. At night, of course, I would dream about them and have nightmares as a result.

Round about this time I was getting prepared for my

First Holy Communion by kind nuns of the Ursuline order in Thurles. I loved this preparation for, I was learning something about religion and the wonders of God, and I had forgotten what little I had learnt about religion when my parents were living in Mulatty. Now my interest was being rekindled by the kind sisters. I was pleased and awed when I was told about the sacrament of Holy Communion.

3

About a year after my First Communion, my parents moved up to County Mayo for the summer months to earn a living. At the time we were travelling with Martin and Minnie Taylor and their only child Sonny. Martin Taylor was a man who never drank and he said that he would go fifty-fifty with whatever he and my father bought and sold. But he made it a condition that my father take the Pledge. My father did in fact do so. Every day they travelled the country selling lino and delf and buying old rags and feathers, horsehair and so on. As well as this they bought old hens and resold them at a handsome profit. In all, we travelled with them for about twelve months and during that time my father never touched a drink. The result was that he and my mother saved a few hundred pounds as well as buying a new wagon and two good horses.

A very profitable and happy partnership indeed it turned out to be. I loved being with the Taylors, for myself and Sonny Taylor, a lad a year older than me, had become very close friends; in fact we were inseparable. We even slept together in our own little tent, which Martin Taylor gave us.

Whilst Martin and my father drove the country in one cart, Sonny and I would drive our mothers in another to mooch the country for the grub-stakes. On these drives Sonny and I became expert moochers and hawkers, especially in the towns.

There was, of course, one great weakness about the Taylor family – superstition and a belief in ghosts. Anything with a hint of being haunted or out of the ordinary frightened Minnie, especially after dark. During our travels with the Taylors my parents were to get many a laugh out of this weakness of theirs. It all started, not at night, but on a bright summer's day, a day that I will never forget for its sheer hilarity.

On this day the two carts were travelling through the country. My father and Martin Taylor were in one cart and my mother, Minnie, Sonny and I in the other, with my small sister and brother as well. It was about one o'clock and the families decided to drum up by the road-side to make a bit of dinner. Minnie said she would go up to the house in the fields, which we could see from the road. The house was a very long way up, but she said she would walk so that the horses could do a bit of grazing. My mother offered to go with her but Minnie said no, she would go up herself.

'It looks like a good house,' said Minnie, 'and I might get a bit of carny and a few roomógs for the dinner. I won't be long. You'll have the fountie boiled up by the time I get back.'

With that, Minnie walked up the long lane to the house; when she got there she went to the front door, which was half open. She did not bother to knock but stepped inside the door casually. When she entered, she found the place dark on account of her coming in from the strong sunshine. She saw the outline of what she thought was a woman standing in front of the fireplace.

'Good day and God bless you, ma'am,' said Minnie. 'It's a nice day we're having now, thank God. I was wondering if...'

Minnie could say no more, for, as soon as the 'woman' turned round, she took full flight out of the door and down the lane as fast as her legs could carry her, screaming her head off. As she ran down the lane she looked back once or twice and this made her scream even louder, for the person who was in the house was running after her, waving her hands and shouting something or other.

At last Minnie arrived to where the rest of us were making the tea. We had become very alarmed when we heard her screaming and saw her running. My father and Martin ran to meet her to see what was wrong. However, when they got Minnie to the cart she fainted.

A few minutes later a man – or what appeared to be a man – came up to us. We recognised him directly as being a bit of a simpleton. He was wearing a long dress-like smock over his trousers and he had a stick with a balloon on the end, which he was waving like a child. Grunting or gurgling was the only kind of noise he made. In all, a harmless fellow; shortly after his arrival his mother came and said she was sorry for her son's behaviour.

'He's very childish in his outlook, and when I heard that woman screaming I got a terrible fright; I hope the poor woman is all right – I can imagine the fright she must have got. My son always gets excited when anyone visits our house. He likes to show off.'

'Bedad, ma'am,' said Martin, 'he picked the wrong woman to show off to when he picked my wife. She is a nervous wreck at the best of times, let alone a time like this. I only hope to God that this fright she got from your son, God bless him, doesn't affect her.'

'When I get back to the house I will send someone down with some meat and eggs for you all. Come with Mumsie, Lambeen,' she cooed to her son as she led him away.

About half an hour later a young girl came down carrying a big bag and gave it to my mother, who opened it after thanking the girl. In it was a side of bacon and about four dozen of eggs. My mother was delighted, as were the menfolk. Minnie was just recovering from her fainting spell and sat up and took in all that was going on around her. 'Thank God,' she said, 'I'm safe, I thought that madman had got me.'

'What madman!' yelled Martin. 'You're raving, woman, raving. That was no madman, but a poor gomey, God bless the mark. A poor innocent and harmless gomey.'

'Gomey, my eye,' said Minnie, 'look Martin, I'm no idiot, I know a gomey when I see one. That was a raving madman that chased me with that axe in his hand. Don't tell me I'm blind because I saw the axe with my own two eyes, and I know one when I see it, just as I know a gomey when I see one.'

'Look, Minnie, there's no good going on about this any more, so let it rest, will you,' said Martin.

'It's easy for you to talk, you were safe; you weren't the one that was nearly killed by your so-called gomey,' said Minnie, who now began to sob.

'Oh for goodness sake, Minnie, buck up girl, you're making me a laughing-stock on the road, you and your wild notions.'

'Yes, Minnie,' my father butted in, 'everything's all right now and you're safe, thank God, so it's best forgotten about; there's no use in husband and wife arguing. I know you got a bad fright but it's finished with now, so let's all get a bit of peck into us, in the name of God.'

That night, when my mother was putting the children to bed, I was full of questions about the episode with Minnie that day.

'Mammy,' I asked, 'why is Minnie so scared? Was she really killed today?'

'No, son, of course not,' answered my mother, 'but you must remember that poor Minnie is a very nervous woman.'

'But why, Mammy?' I asked. 'What made her nervous?'

'She got a bad fright when she was very young, that's why,' replied my mother.

'Were you there when she got the fright, Mammy?' I asked cunningly.

'Yes, I was indeed, son.'

'Tell us about it, Mammy, please tell us.'

'Well, years ago, when Minnie and I were little girls,' my mother began, 'our families travelled the road together for a number of years. The time that Minnie got the fright we were travelling in the West of Ireland. My father and mother had only a tent, as had Minnie's parents.

'Anyway, one evening we had pulled into a little-known camping ground and made a bit of supper before the camps were to be put down. During the supper Minnie's mother, Lord rest her soul, took bad. To make matters worse, we were right out in the wilds, miles from the nearest village or town. It was decided, however, that both our families would travel to the nearest town that night instead of camping in the wilds. They knew that Minnie's mother needed a doctor, and in those days doctors would not travel to tend a pavvy.

'Anyhow,' continued my mother, 'we packed up, and with all of us in our respective carts we set off at a good trot for the nearest town. It was a lovely night, though a small bit cold, and you could see for miles in the bright moonlight. We travelled along for hours – days it seemed to me – and the younger kids fell asleep and were covered up in the carts. Everything was quiet except for the murmuring of our parents' chat and the old shriek of a curlew of plover or distant bark of a dog; all was deadly silent.

'Along we jogged, but the road seemed to be getting longer and longer and Minnie's mother began to get worse, which caused great worry to her father and my mother and father – Lord have mercy on them all, we mustn't forget to say a prayer for them after we finish this story,' interrupted my mother.

'Well, to continue, we came at last to an old railway bridge which crossed over the roadway and, the Lord save us, things began to happen suddenly.

'First, as we got to the bridge, the cart in front of us stopped and our cart stopped too. "What's up?" my father asked Big Jim (as Minnie's dad was called).

' "I don't know, Tom," said Big Jim, "the horse won't move, I think he's winded."

'"Well let me out in front, Jim, then he might follow," said my father.'

'"All right then, pull out and see," said Jim.

'My father, God rest his soul, then gave our old horse a clout and started to pull him out. But he too would not budge. My father gave him a great few wallops with a stick but he still would not move.

'"Jim, there's something wrong with the old animals, mine won't even move an inch," said my father. "I think we'll get down and try to lead them; they might be shy of the bridge."

'"Okay, let's do that," said Big Jim, "and, even better still, we can put something over their heads to blindfold them."

' "A good idea," said my father.

'So they put an old sack over each pony's head, then led them past the bridge. And, strangely enough, it worked; the ponies moved and, when they got past the bridge, the two men took the sacks off the horses' heads – and got back into the carts. Then, God save us from all harm, strange things began to happen on that lonely road, that terrible night. Barely had my dad and Minnie's got back on their carts when the both of the horses bolted. The more our fathers tried to pull them up, the more useless it became. The horses were racing at full gallop. Of course our fathers were so worried about what was happening that they could not speak to each other. The only thing they could do was to let the horses have their heads, hoping that they would soon tire of their sudden galloping fever.

'They had got about a mile from the bridge when young Minnie began to scream unmercifully. "Don't take Mammy, don't take Mammy!" she roared, then suddenly stopped screaming.

'So, too, did the horses stop their tracks. My father jumped down off our cart and ran to Jim's to see what the shouting was about. "What's wrong, Jim? Who was screaming?" he asked.'

'"Oh, it's Minnie shouting, she must've been having a nightmare, but it looks like she's asleep again," said Jim. "The wife is asleep as well, and it's a good job too. If she had to have seen the way the horses behaved it might have given her a bad turn."'

'"Thank God for that, I thought something really bad had happened when I heard them ear-splitting screams," said my father.

'My father then remarked to Jim, "Bedad, Jim, your old horse is in a lather of sweat and he's shaking too."

'"Yeah," said Jim, "it must've been that run he had; I expect yours'll be the same. I can't figure out what made them run so, though, unless they took fright at the bridge. All I can say is they certainly travelled that bit of the road."

'"Yes," said my father, "they got a fright of some kind, and my horse is sweating too, but I bet he won't run much now. Still, we're not far from the town so we can take it steady."

'With that we set off again, this time at a walk. My father asked me to get under the cover and try to get some sleep, but I wouldn't. I did not feel sleepy. Besides, my father and Jim, and I think everyone else, had fallen asleep again. A few had been woken by Minnie's screams but soon dropped off to sleep again.

'Anyway, when we reached the town, about an hour later, my father woke my mother up, and they went with Jim to the garda station to find out about a doctor. I was told to keep an eye on the rest and not to wake them up.

'About half an hour later they came back with a garda, a doctor and a nurse. The doctor went straight to Jim's cart to examine his wife. He pulled back the cover to examine Minnie's mother; within a matter of seconds he put the cover back over her face and whispered something hurriedly to the nurse and the garda. Then he turned to Jim and said, "I'm deeply sorry, sir, but your wife is dead and has been so for two or three hours I should say. It's obvious, too, that you did not know that."

'I shall never forget the way poor Big Jim broke down when the doctor told him. He roared just like a child. My own mother and father too were deeply shocked. The nurse said that if they could try not to disturb the children now it would be a great help. In fact, she advised Jim not to say anything to them for a day or two.

'Shortly afterwards an ambulance came, and the remains of Jim's wife were taken away to hospital. A few days later she was buried and all of us attended the funeral. It disturbed Jim and his children a great deal; they had to be given sedatives to calm their grief after the funeral.

'Well, children,' my mother continued, 'I was only a slip of a girl, but I felt very sorry for Minnie and her family over their great loss. A few days later we learned that she had died of a tumour. We learned too that she had suffered for some time without letting on to anyone. What a fine and loving mother she was. She must have known she was going to die, but would not say anything about it to worry her husband and children; God rest her poor soul, sure she is in Heaven, poor woman.

'After the funeral we stayed travelling with Jim and his children; my own mother said this would be the best thing to do until they got over their grieving. We all moved away straight after the funeral and headed back the way we came.

'Well children, we are coming to the puzzling part of the story now. When we got nearer to the place where the horses ran away we – well, my father and mother and Big Jim anyway – got a bit of shock, for on the road on either side there were some crosses marking the spot where some people had been killed during the troubles in Ireland. The first one was about a mile from the railway bridge and the last very close to the bridge itself.

'"Are you thinking what I'm thinking?" said Big Jim to my father.

'"Bedad, I am," said my father, "this is a haunted road. We did not see anything that night but our horses did and that's why they ran away."

' "That's right," replied Jim, "and to make matters worse I think that then, or at the time the horses bolted, my dear wife died, Lord have mercy on her. I feel sure now that this road was the undoing of her."

' "I would not like to think so, Jim, but something very mysterious happened the night we came along this road. What it really was we shall never know. What a great loss to you, the death of your wife, a good woman indeed; may she rest in peace."

' "Well, Tom, the only thing I can do is to get as far away as possible from this road and never come near it again. It will always hold bad memories for me."

'Well, to finish,' said my mother, 'young Minnie was very affected by the death of her mother, and, for all we know –

though she never said a word about it – she too saw something that night. I do know that for weeks after her mother's death Minnie hardly spoke one word; she was moping all the time, as if she was in a kind of trance. Whatever it was, Minnie was never the same. To this very day she is very nervous indeed, especially at night. So there you are now, that's the story about Minnie.'

'I think,' said I, who had listened in awe, 'that it was very sad for Minnie, having no mother.'

'Yes,' said my mother, 'and you should say a prayer for Minnie so that she will get over her bad nerves.'

'I will anyhow,' I said, 'because I like Minnie.'

'All right then children, away to bed now because it's terrible late to be talking about the dead of the past,' said my mother.

Thus I was to dream again of ghosts and spirits, and of Minnie, in my sleep that night. I loved these tales, and even though I often became scared listening to them, I still loved them. A week or so after this story had been told by my mother I was to witness once again Minnie's imagination running rife.

It was a clear evening, though getting dark, when Minnie was asked by her husband to get some water for the morning. Minnie did not even argue in any way, but just grabbed the can and went to fetch it. After all, she had to go only a hundred yards or so up the road to the house to get it. In fact, the house was in sight of the camp-fire. No one took a bit of notice as she left the fire.

Ten minutes or so later, however, everyone was running towards the house when they heard the unmerciful screams of Minnie as she came tearing down the road. When she arrived at the fireside she fainted.

Neither my parents nor Minnie's husband could get any sense out of her mumbles as to what, if anything, had happened to her. My father and Minnie's husband went up to the house to see what happened. I sneaked up after them with nothing but my shirt on. When we got to the house everything was dead quiet. There was no light in the farmhouse window, so the two men took it to mean that the people of the house were out somewhere or in bed. They went to the shed where there was a little hand pump. The front of the shed was completely open on the very verge of the roadside. They found the water can on the ground near the pump. The two men then examined the shed with a little torch that my father had in his pocket. All they could see in the shed were two old carts with four or five turkeys roosting on them.

'I can't see what frightened her here,' said my father, 'she must be imagining things, or if there was anything it's gone now, and there's nothing we can do.'

'I don't know,' said Minnie's husband, 'unless she got frightened by the turkeys, but Minnie wouldn't be frightened of them.'

'What on earth are you doing here, Sean?' said my father when he saw me. He caught me and gave me a few slaps on the bare legs. 'You won't follow us again in your shirt, you little cur you.'

With that I ran home crying.

When the men got back to the camp they could get no coherent words from Minnie so they went to bed, to leave the matter until the morning.

The next morning Minnie was all right again and she told everyone about what had happened the night before. 'Well,' she said, 'I went to the shed for the water, and, as I was putting the can under the pump, I heard footsteps behind me. I turned around and there I saw four or five terrible faces staring at me; they were all dressed in black and began talking in very strange voices. Well, all I know,' she continued, 'is that I took to my heels as fast as ever I could, and thank God that I did. I'm not surprised that they were gone when you went there.'

'Well,' said her husband, 'Minnie, my love, I've got news for you; the four or so terrible faces you saw are still there and, if you want to, you can come and see them in the daylight for yourself. But let me tell you first that what you saw were some harmless turkeys roosting for the night. Nothing else.'

'Listen, Martin,' said Minnie, 'it's no good you trying to ease my mind. I know you are trying to help me by this simple explanation, but you forget that I know what a turkey is and if they were turkeys I saw last night, then they are the first ones I have heard of who wear boots, and wear clothes – black clothes – and speak a funny language. No Martin, they may have changed into turkeys when you and Mickeen got there. But they were men in black that I saw.'

'Well, Mickeen,' said Martin, 'we can't win, and it's useless trying to.'

'Ah well, Martin,' said Mickeen, 'Minnie has got over it now, thank God, so there's nothing to worry about.'

'You're right, indeed, Mickeen,' said Martin, 'there's no good in going any further with the matter; my wife is getting worse with her imagination, instead of better. Turkeys with boots on! What next!' he added with irony.

What next, indeed. I learned a lot about the fears of Martin as well as Minnie during the period when we travelled together. I laughed my head off at some bizarre, so-called happenings to Minnie and Martin. My parents too got great enjoyment from listening to their antics. At times my father, especially when there were other travellers with us, would deliberately concoct some scheme to scare Martin and Minnie. One such scheme was laid on by my father and some other travellers. It was a simple one but one that was far from funny for poor Martin and Minnie and was eventually to end in a punch-up.

My father and another traveller, Willie MacFageon, hatched the plot whilst Martin and Minnie were in town. Their wagon was parked near a large tree with huge overhanging branches which reached quite low over the top of the wagon. They got a reel of very strong thread; Willie climbed onto one of the low-lying branches and tied the thread, with plenty of slack, to the top of the wagon just over the door. He then climbed back onto the tree-branch, unreeling the thread as he climbed back down on the ground again. The trunk of the tree stood behind the rather large hedge that ran alongside the wagon. 'Well,' said my dad, 'did you fix it so it won't tangle when we pull it?'

'Yes,' said Willie, 'It'll do the trick grand; I'd like to try it out but that would be hard as they might come any minute and catch us in the act. I feel sure though that it'll work all right. Tonight I'll go into their wagon and on the way out connect the thread to that knocker of theirs.'

'Yes,' said my Dad, 'I'll be behind this edge listening to the fun.'

'We'd better get out of here now or they might come and catch us,' said Willie; 'you can't notice the thread, Mickeen, can you?'

'Not a sight, Willie lad, not a glimpse of it through them leaves,' said my father.

That night, at half ten or so, Willie went to Martin's wagon and found that they were getting ready for bed. He asked, as an excuse, for some matches. Martin obliged by giving him a few and bade him good night. Willie stepped back out, closing the door after him, and as he did so he reached up for the thread and looped it quickly around the knocker. He got back to my father's place which was about a hundred yards down the road.

'Everything all right?' asked my father.

'Gameball, Mickeen, gameball,' said Willie.

'Well we'll just have to wait a while now and then we'll have some fun,' said my father.

And wait they did, for about two hours or so. They weren't the only ones, however. Myself and Tiny, Willie's eleven-year-old son, were also waiting. We had overheard our fathers plotting and decided that we would sneak after them and watch the fun without being seen.

When things seemed ripe enough, my father and Willie climbed through the hedge and walked down behind it until they came to the big tree. We weren't far behind them, but were well hidden so they couldn't see us. My father and Willie waited and listened for about ten minutes; they could plainly hear light snoring coming from the wagon.

'Now is the time,' whispered Willie, 'but for goodness sake keep your voice to the whisper, and, another thing, we mustn't laugh out loud or we'll spoil the whole thing.'

'Okay,' whispered my father, 'you pull the thread and then release it quickly.'

The result was perfect; they could hear the dead thud of the knocker as it hit the door. Willie waited a few seconds before he repeated the act. He did this for about five minutes or so, making sure to leave a good space between each knock for effect and also to hear what was or would be said in the wagon. Very soon they heard the voice of Minnie, and when they did they stopped the knocking.

'Martin,' they could plainly hear her saying, 'are you awake?'

'Yes, woman, how could anyone sleep with someone nudging him in the back with an elbow?'

'Listen, Martin, I've been hearing knocking on the door for the past half hour or so.'

'It must be your head that's knocking, then,' said Martin.

'Look, Martin, I tell you it was knocking I heard.'

'All right then, go to the door and see who it is that's knocking, and that'll be the end of that,' said Martin.

'Listen, Martin, it was no human knocking that I heard, it was the dead man's knocking.'

'Well, dead man or live man,' shouted Martin, 'I've heard nothing and neither have you other than your imagin – what's that?'

'I told you, Mr Braveman, that's the knocking I was telling you about.'

'Oh shut up, woman,' said Martin angrily, 'and let me listen.'

Outside my father and Willie had begun the knocking again.

'Minnie, will you go to the door and see who's knocking?'

'Not for the life of me, Martin, will I stir from my bed this unholy night,' Minnie said, and then started to pray aloud.

'Who's there?' shouted Martin towards the door. 'Who's that knocking? In the name of God answer before my wife dies of fright, whoever you are!'

'It's no good,' said Martin, 'I'll have to get up and see what's wrong before you drive me barmy, you and your dead man's knock!'

With that, Martin got out of the bed and went and opened the door, and, as luck would have it for my father and Willie, Martin only opened the bottom of the door, leaving the upper half closed.

'Well, woman,' shouted Martin, 'are you pleased now? Look out and you'll see, with your own gawky eyes, that there's no one there. Can I go back now and get a night's sleep? Or is it asking too much?'

'That's right, you dirty coward you, put the blame on me again,' said Minnie angrily. 'You always make sure to disbelieve me, when you hear it yourself.'

'Listen, Minnie, for goodness sake, I'm only trying to tell you that there *was* knocking; but it was probably an old dog or something which was making the noise,' answered Martin.

'Dog? There must be funny dogs around these parts, if they can reach up and knock on the door,' said Minnie.

'Okay, Minnie, you win, it was a dead man; now let me get back to sleep, seeing that our ghostly knocker no longer knocks!'

So back to bed they went and started to settle down again. Meanwhile, my father and Willie were near bursting with laughter for they could hear every word that was being said in the wagon. Myself and Tiny were enjoying this haunting escapade, too, not very far away. After another quarter of an hour or so Willie started to knock again. Again Minnie was the first to hear it.

'Martin, love, there's your dog knocking again,' she said with sarcasm. 'My, but that dog of yours has a deadly knock.'

'Minnie, don't keep on, will you give your tongue a rest?' asked Martin.

'Yes, Yes!' she shouted, 'but don't you hear that knocking, are you deaf?'

'No, I'm not deaf, but at times I wish I was,' said

Martin. 'Of course I hear knocking, but what can I do if there's no one there?'

'Well, if it's the dog you said that's knocking, you can give him that old bone out of the press and he might go!' said Minnie in sheer sarcasm.

It was at the end of these words that Tiny and I burst out laughing. Our laughter could be heard plainly in the wagon.

'There,' said Martin, 'there's your deadman's knock, or the ghostly knockers – them young lads from the other camp. Well, I'll give them knocking when I get these clothes on!'

About ten minutes or so later, after the discovery of the thread, Martin and Minnie went up to the other camp to get chastisement put on the two brats who were so wicked in trying to scare a poor nervous woman. When they got to the other camp they found everyone tucked away, apparently asleep. This, however, did not convince Minnie and Martin, who immediately began roaring abuse out on the road. My father and Willie jumped out of their beds, looking quite innocent, and tried to pacify the roaring loonies on the road. They nearly ended up in punch-up, because my father and Willie were trying to protect us from being attacked by Martin and Minnie.

The following day Martin and Minnie moved away, having had enough pranks played on them. I missed them, because I had come to like them. I wasn't all that pleased with my father and Willie for the trick they played on them. At the time it was funny but, when I thought about it later, I felt sorry for them. On my travels, however, I too often saw ill-treatment of humans and animals alike. This was part and parcel of the road-life, something that I was powerless to stop or even lessen. This part of my destiny was to bring many pitfalls, many joys, sorrows and very little triumph.

4

In the spring of 1943, I was eleven years old and an expert at making a living on the road, by way of begging, selling and chanting the gat-ceans. Each morning I would leave the molly with my little basket of swag to hawk the country. Now the basket contained many little articles such as ballad sheets, shoe-laces, little holy statues and rosary beads, holy pictures, cups, tin mugs and artificial flowers.

The entire contents of the basket were bought wholesale for about one pound or thirty shillings. The flowers and tin mugs were made by my parents. Most of our swag was bought in bulk, for my father would buy ten or twelve pounds' worth at a time.

The most famous place for buying our swag then was still the 'Monster House' in Kilkenny. The manager at that time was very kind to the travellers and always sold them articles for less than his settled customers paid. There too, my father would buy rolls of lino, glassware, little pictures, crêpe-paper (to make flowers) and many other articles. When all was purchased he would pack the lot into two large wicker baskets with one handle across the top, so as to make it easy for him to carry it over his arm. It was such baskets that we carried around with us, only they were much smaller.

The ballad sheets we bought came from Listowel and from Cahirciveen. We used to buy the ballads in bulk, five hundred or a thousand sheets of very varied songs, and always asked for more sheets of the most popular song at the time. Around this time ballad sheets cost us about seven-and-sixpence per five hundred sheets; we, in turn, would sell them at a minimum of threepence each; this was a very useful and profitable little trade indeed.

To sell my wares I often covered eight or ten miles on foot in a day, very often getting home quite late at night.

My method of selling, so I was told, was very good. I had a way of appealing to people, who would give me something before I left their door, even if they bought none of my wares.

Begging, of course, was an instinct with me as well as an art. But then, all travellers are endowed with the art of begging. No matter what I earned by begging in a day, I would still want more.

When out begging or hawking my approach to a cean was always the same. I would go to the back or side door in preference to the front. If I were to knock at the front door, the occupier might look out the window and, seeing a traveller, decide not to answer the door, so that going to one of the other doors would catch the occupier unawares.

When the door was answered to my knock, I always began in the same old way: 'Good day, ma'am, it's not a bad day, thank God. Well, missus, I wonder if you would be interested in some of my wares today? I have a different stock to the last time I was here.'

'What do you mean, the last time you were here? Are you codding me or something? Sure I never saw you before,' would be the usual reply. However, I soon talked my way around this type of situation. Then, as often as not, the person of the house would say, 'Well, what have you got, anyway?'

As soon as I was asked this I was in. I had my mark (buyer); I would then say, 'Well, ma'am,' as I moved into the house, 'let me put me basket on your table so that you can have a good look at my wares. I won't charge you anything for looking at them.' Nine times out of ten I would make a sale; then I would start to mooch. 'Could you give us a bit of tea and sugar or a bit of meat to take home, ma'am? And may God bless you.' The kinder the person of the house was the more I would beg, for I knew that a soft touch was hard to find.

To meet such a kind person was to make their particular house a very good mark. Such good marks were to be remembered for future calls. The phrase 'good mark' or 'bad mark' came about by an easy landmark of the house being taken down and noted. So that whenever we talked about the house in our own family we would say, 'the long laned house', 'the broken wall house', 'the threshing engine house', or the 'house with the blind comeragh'. The bad houses or bad marks were always described by something abusive of its occupants. Thus you had bad houses called: 'the humpy woman's', 'the scutchy beor's' or 'the ruilla feen's cean'. All had their various names.

Each travelling family had their own good and bad marks and would call to every good mark at various intervals throughout the year. The bad marks were always avoided. All too often, though, what might prove to be a bad mark to one travelling family might be a good mark to another family. Houses throughout Ireland, especially the farmhouses, were like this, and always had their own cronies among the travelling people.

This is why we pavvies have a liking for particular towns and parts of the country. For it is around such places that we make the best living. Any such good mark that we have is to be respected, and woe betide any of our family who clammed such good marks by abuse or impudence. It would mean a good corrupting from our father. 'Never connia on your own jigger' is a vulgar expression which really means 'Never dirty your own door'.

My family had a great number of good marks in Clare and Galway and I too had many in these counties. In fact, at some of my marks, where I got clothes, food and money without any trouble, the same houses would chase my parents or brothers and sisters or anyone else.

We only travelled these counties in the summer. At nearly every house I would go to, especially in the evenings when the whole household was home, I would be brought in so that the people could have a chat with me.

'Come in, creature, so we can look you, won't you?' was the usual greeting. 'Well, me little gosoon, where on earth did you hail from and what's your name?' I would be asked.

'Me name's John Devine, but my parents call me Sean for short,' I would answer.

'And why wouldn't they, creature? Sure Sean is a grand name, God bless you,' would be their answer.

'Are you hungry, son?' I would answer 'Yes', and I would then be given some tea, or even dinner, if it was during the day. I would often be invited to sit at the table and eat supper with the whole family of the house, during which I would be showered with all kinds of questions. I would readily answer all, and in turn would ask quite a few myself. People took to me immediately, mainly because of my childish curiosity and talkativeness. I would never tire of talking.

'Do you like the road, Sean?' would be a favourite question asked of me.

'No, not really, ma'am,' was always my answer. 'I would rather live in a house.'

'But why, alannah?' I would be asked. 'Isn't road life grand and free and easy?'

'It is, ma'am, in the good weather, but not in the bad,' I would reply. 'Besides that, ma'am, I would like to be able to go to school and I can't do that when we're travelling.'

'Arrah, off with you! What schooling do you need?' was too often the answer I got. 'Sure you will have time enough for that later. Besides, what would you do if you did get schooling, I mean when you finished school?'

'Oh that's easy,' I used to answer, 'I would become a priest or a monk, and then I could help my parents and brothers and sisters.'

This simple answer always brought a smile to the faces of my hearers, who would often say:

'Fancy that now, Sean wants to be a priest; imagine having a tinker priest!'

Remarks like this always made me angry; although they were not made out of disrespect, I didn't like them.

'Look, ma'am,' I would reply to such remarks, 'I'm not a tinker, I'm a traveller, and our Blessed Lord himself was a traveller, ma'am.'

'Ah no child, we meant no disrespect to you when we said that,' would be the apologetic reply. 'In fact it would be good to have a traveller priest. But, tell us, alannah, who told you that Our Lord was a traveller?' I would be asked next.

'My mother,' was my reply. 'She told us, and it's true too, that Our Lord used to travel around all the time. She told us that even when he was born his parents had to sleep in an old shed.'

'Why, poor child, you are right, and your poor mother is right too,' was the reply.

I used to love, though, to sit and chat with the people in the houses. Indeed I often spent hours in this way.

After wandering through the country earning my few mideogs, I would all too often arrive home late. When I did I had to be prepared for the greeting I always got. I would have to have all I collected and begged accounted for so that whenever I reached home I was always greeted in the same manner:

'Hallo, son, whatever kept you till this hour? I was getting very worried about you.'

'Oh, I had to walk a good bit, Mammy,' I replied.

'Well, come and sit down, son, and I'll make you a drop of weed. How did you get on today, creature? You look tired.'

'Oh, I didn't do too bad, I got about three pounds mooching and a good bit of food there in the bag. Here's the money, and remember, don't give Daddy any of it. Where is Daddy by the way? In the pub as usual, I suppose?'

'Yes, he has gone to the town, but he can't really help it son, because drink is like a disease and he can't do without it. You must not be too hard; after all, he is your father.'

'I know that, Mammy, but I would love him to stop drinking, then he wouldn't beat you and the rest of us. You should not let him see the money or let him know how much we give you. You could get someone to mind, or save, the money for you – like a nun or a priest.'

'However did you learn about saving, child? What put that idea in your young head?'

'Oh, a woman in a house told me this, she said this way the money wouldn't be spent foolishly on drink.'

'It's a good idea, son, but it would be very hard to do, because we keep moving all the time; anyway, we have to spend the most of it on food because we don't always get enough from begging, as you well know.'

'Oh, Mammy, I hope God makes Daddy stop drinking, then I would like him, but I can't like him when he is drinking, especially when he beats you. Oh, Mammy, why does Daddy hate me, why does he be so cruel to us all?'

'You mustn't talk like that, son. God and his Blessed Mother love all poor travelling people and when we pray hard enough he will help us; you must remember that prayer is never lost. So have your supper now, child, and then get some sleep and everything will be all right.'

'Mammy?'

'What, son?'

'I wish we could live in a house again, like other people do; I bet we would be happy then.'

'I wish so too, son, but we would starve in a house because your father would never be able to get a job. Times are very bad these days for people living in houses, because of the war and all. Work is very, very scarce. If we were to stay in a house it would be worse for us, because we are classed as tinkers. But one day soon, please God, when you and your brothers and sisters are a little bigger, we'll be able to get a house.'

'That would be no good, Mammy, we wouldn't be able to go to school then, because we would be too big!'

'Well, in the name of God, what brought school into your mind? Sure you wouldn't like to go to school, would you? I don't know where you get these funny notions from child, honest I don't. School! what next, I ask you, child.'

'But, Mammy, I do want to go to school, and the priests and nuns told me I should, to learn to read and write. All children, except travelling children, can go to school and they get free food and clothes there too – schoolboys told me so.'

'That's all very well, son, people in houses can get these things, but us poor unfortunates on the road can't. And, as I said, we can't get a house straight away, it takes a long time to get one. But one day, please God, we'll have a house to live in and then you'll be all right, so pray that we will be able to get one soon. Now, off to bed before your Daddy comes, you know what he is like when he gets home; so get into bed out of his way!'

'Mammy, could I not get a little tent of my own, 'cause I don't like sleeping in the big tent listening to Daddy arguing all night for nothing. I hate when night comes and I do be glad when it's morning and I can get away for the day again.'

'But why let that worry you, son – sleeping with us all in the tent I mean? I know your father is contrary betimes, but don't we all get over that? You shouldn't take these things to heart too much, you know, after all, we are for your own good!'

'I know, Mammy, I love you very much, but I do be lonely and I never have pals or anything; all I hear is rows and arguments all the time. The thing I hate most, though, is the loneliness.'

'Don't be soft, child, for goodness sake, you have no need to be lonely. Haven't you your brothers and sisters to play with?'

'I know, Mammy, but it's not the same as having pals, like Twister and Ghosty and others. These are the kind of pals I mean; I get tired playing with my brothers and sisters, because they are there all the time, night and day. Even when I go mooching I go mostly on my own and then I really feel lonely. If we could be with other travellers all the time the road wouldn't be too bad.'

'Ah, well son, we'll soon meet some travellers again and things will be all right, but you must remember it isn't always possible to be with other travellers because mooching would be twice as hard; with two families travelling together we would have opposition.'

'Mammy, when you were young, were you ever lonely?'

'Yes, of course I was, at times, but I got over it. I didn't let it worry me, like it does you. You must remember that when I was your age, the road was a lot more lonely than it is today. There was no such a thing as pictures to go to, or cars and cycles like there are today. Oh yes indeed, the old days on the road were far lonelier and much less hospitable, especially during the troubles.'

'Mammy, how long have the tinkers been travelling the road? I got told that they have been on the road for thousands of years. Is this true or not?'

'Well son, I would not say thousands but I would say hundreds, and a good few hundred at that.'

'How did it start, Mammy? Why did people take to the road?'

'This I don't really know son, but I do know that, at the time of St Patrick, there were many travellers in Ireland. Indeed, it was they who helped St Patrick when he was a boy slave. They smuggled him away from his cruel master, because the travellers hated any form of slavery or being tied down to settled life.'

'Mammy, this might have been a made-up story about St Patrick.'

'So it might, but I'll tell you one thing, I believe it; I know that this and other stories are passed down from generation to generation among the travellers, and they are not people who add to tales themselves. You must remember that the records of deeds in the past are always passed down by word of mouth. From listening at camp-fires when stories are told, you will know what great attention is given to detail. I have heard a story at one camp-fire and maybe years later I have heard the same story at another, the important details still unchanged. You must remember that story-telling is our only means of communication with the past. We on the road can't write our deeds, but we do remember them and pass them down faithfully by word of mouth.'

'Do the ordinary people know about St Patrick being helped by travellers?'

'Indeed, son, they don't, for all their education and books; they don't even know where St Patrick came from, or when. If it weren't for the travellers, and the few scraps written by St Patrick himself, they would know nothing at all about him.'

'Mammy, will you tell us the story about St Patrick and the travellers because I've never heard it? All the children are asleep and I'll be company for you until Daddy gets back; you know he'll be very late as usual.'

'Yes, I suppose you're right; I hope nothing has happened to him because that man is a pure idiot when he's drunk. He might walk under a car or fall into a river or something, God forbid. I'll tell you, but as soon as you hear him coming, scoot off into bed.'

'I will, Mammy, don't you worry.'

'Well, wherever Patrick came from, he ended up a captive shepherd in the Northlands of Ireland. It was as such whilst attending sheep on a mountainside that Patrick first came in contact with Ireland's travelling people. It is said that a little travelling lad was the first to come in contact with him while he was out gathering sticks to make a fire.

'This little lad used go to the mountain-side to chat or play with Patrick without saying a word to his parents or anyone. The boy, I suppose, did not think it necessary. One day, however, he mentioned it to his mother, when she asked him where he was going and, especially, why he was taking some food with him.

'The boy said casually that he was going to take it to his pal who talked very funny. His mother instantly became curious and asked more questions. The little boy told her about Patrick minding the sheep on the mountainside.

'The little boy's mother then told him to bring his pal Patrick back with him for a bit of supper. The little boy went to where he was and, by signs and a little Irish, asked Patrick to come home with him for some supper. Patrick, as best he could, told the boy that he could not do that as his master would beat him something terrible if he left the sheep.

'Anyway, a little time later, Patrick eventually went to the boy's camp, where he found great hospitality. A few weeks later the child's mother decided that the best thing for Patrick to do was to come away with them travelling, when it was hoped that Patrick might eventually make his way to France. It was hoped too that he might trace his parents or relatives. At any rate he would end his slave days.

'With these plans in mind Patrick stayed with the travellers for some time, during which he came to know and love all he met on the road. About six months or so later, Patrick made his way to the Continent, where he spent the remainder of his youth learning and studying for the priesthood.

'Around the year 432 or so Patrick returned to Ireland, this time a bishop and Christ's shepherd. When Patrick returned to Ireland he went back on the road with the travellers. In fact, it was to them that he first preached the words of Christ. In this way it was the travellers who became his disciples, and especially the man who had been the little boy that first met him many years before.

'Of course, in those far-off days, Ireland had its castles and forts, for it had many kings and most of the people were well-off; but not so the travellers; they were still on the move in their makeshift tents, not much different from those of today. It was with these that Patrick travelled around Ireland preaching the word of God, succeeding eventually in converting the nation to Christianity. So you see, in St Patrick the travellers had a very special friend as well as a saint, and for this we should always be thankful and very mindful of him in our prayers.'

'That was a beautiful story, Mammy; I wish I could hear stories like that always. I could sit listening to that one for years and years.'

I became more and more interested in learning and anxious for my parents to settle down. This need to settle down became an obsession with me. Strolling through the countryside on my own, my thoughts became deeper. I had no-one in whom to confide them. Time and time again I asked my parents but was never able to get satisfying answers. Thus on my lonely wanderings I would ask questions, in my boyish way, of my Maker.

I shortened my journey home with these boyish chats. Already I was mystified by the world and the wonders about me. I was thinking far too deeply for my years and lack of any education. Each day my young brain became more intent on knowing and learning more of the world around me. I became more restless in myself and mystified my parents and those who knew me. My parents could not understand my strangeness and my dislike of road life. As the years moved on they were to become more worried and mystified, and were to experience intense worry and sorrow as a result of my way of thinking.

5

By the time I was twelve years old I was looking at life with the eyes of a boy and examining it with the mind of a man. Road life had forced me to mature before my time, probably because I was looked on as a breadwinner as soon as I was able to beg. I was an expert in this art. There were, of course, other factors which brought about this horrible, premature maturity – like the rows between my father and mother, and the cruel hardships that are part and parcel of road life.

To add further difficulty to my growing up I had become a stranger among the general run of people of the road. There was something about me that always made people on the road pass remarks about my strangeness, although I was well liked by the other travellers, as well as settled people. Time and time again people would say that I was a strange one because I was forever asking questions impossible to answer. It made people anxious to discover why a travelling boy should want to know so much.

Nevertheless, I went on asking questions and seeking answers, and the person most annoyed by this was my own father. He completely lacked any formal education and resented my enquiring mind. For some mysterious reason he showed open resentment of me, mainly because I was not what he expected me to be. 'Why can't you be like the rest of the children? You won't hear them asking silly questions or worrying about going to school. Are you going soft in the head or what?' Such remarks from my father hurt very much. I would keep asking myself why he did not like me. I got the feeling that he hated me a great deal, but I could not understand why.

As the years went by, I became more troubled and puzzled by my father's resentment and his ill-treatment of me. As I went about my business mooching I would often, in the long laneways between country houses, talk to God and have it out with him. 'God, why don't you make my father like me? Why don't you stop him from fighting with my mother over me? She always sticks up for me, but when she does my father beats her. This isn't fair, Lord. Why do you let it happen?'

But even God, it seemed then, hadn't the answer to my questions. I would ask him for a sign, any sign, in acknowledgement of all my prayers, but he never made one that I could recognise as such. And so I would plod back, late at night, to the mollying around.

At one stage I felt that those on the road were a people cursed by God. I would think of the cold days when my feet were cracked open with the cold and the heat of the fire would make them feel worse instead of better. I would visualise grey winter afternoons when the mist hung so low that even a blazing fire failed to keep away the chilling dampness that settled on us.

If it were only summer. I could tolerate the life if summer stretched the year around. Clare or Galway in the month of June would restore my faith in God. Over beyond Gort or Corofin, solitude sang its own hymn. On purple heathered mountains I lay stretched, my breath catching in the summer breezes. Larks would rise their traditional songs and fill whole valleys while a cuckoo mocked them from a bush nearby. Grasshoppers and bees added to, rather than took from, my solitude. The whine of the telegraph poles was as sweet as the tumbling of a waterfall. Even the blue fraughans I picked lost their bitter taste. But even as I revelled in my surroundings I would ask myself: 'Do other boys feel as I do? Am I different from them?' Certainly my companions never admitted to liking the things in nature that I liked.

'Oh, good night, sir.'

'Good night to you, me lad!'

'I beg your pardon, sir, but could you give us a few pennies to get a bit of food and I'll say a prayer for you, will ya?'

'A few pennies to buy food at this time of night?'

'Yes, sir, I'll get the food in the morning!'

'You will, will you? Okay then, here's two shillings, and don't forget the prayer; good night, now, and God bless you.'

'Thank you, sir, I won't forget!'

'That was a nice sham, a few more like him and things would be okay. That reminds me, I must not forget to say the prayer for that man; I will say it now! Hail Mary full of grace, the Lord is with thee... That is for the man who gave me the two shillings and all the people for whom I promised to say a prayer.'

'I'm sorry, God, but I keep forgetting to say a prayer for the people from whom I beg. I know it's not fair and maybe that's why you don't speak to me or help us. I must confess that it is wrong to keep telling people that I will say a prayer for them and then forget all about it. I suppose that this is why you are forgetting us too; is this the reason why you don't seem to help travellers?'

Thus I continued my questions and searches for answers. This questioning and searching brought me still more loneliness, sadness and tears. As I got lonelier and lonelier, I began to think of a way to escape from this. My parents, on the other hand, through sheer ignorance, could not understand the difficult period I was going through. They had a far different answer for my behaviour and this answer was doing far more harm than good.

'Bridie, do you know that Sean is getting more peculiar every day?' I overheard my father say one night.

'What in the name of God is peculiar about Sean, Mickeen? Sure all young lads act funny like Sean betimes; it's the way boys go on, Mickeen, and it's nothing to worry about.'

'Look, Bridie girl, it's not normal for a lad Sean's age – he's nearly twelve now – to be talking to himself. If you ask me I think that he's really soft in the head.'

'Soft in the head, me eye! 'Tis you that's soft in the head, if you think that way about Sean. No, Mickeen, there is nothing at all wrong with Sean; he's a bit lonely now and again 'cause we don't meet many travellers these days and he misses his pals; that's all that's wrong with him.'

'Yes, that's what you say, Bridie. Well, let me tell you something for nothing, then. The other night I was looking for the old pony in a field; as I was walking by the hedge which ran alongside the road I heard Sean having a great chat to himself.

'At first I didn't know what was wrong; I recognised his voice, so I peeped through the hedge to see who he was talking to, only to get the surprise of my life. For there, by the roadside, sat Sean, talking goodoh to himself. I didn't disturb him but listened to every word he said. What I heard that night convinced me that he's getting a bit touched in the head.'

'Touched, my eye, you're imagining things, Mickeen, I tell you there's nothing wrong with Sean. I know for a fact that he's badly in need of a bit of schooling. Nearly everyone passes the same remark about Sean; they all say he is a bright child.'

'That may be, Bridie, but I don't like the way he has taken to religion. When I overheard him he was talking to God. He keeps on about his hate for road-life and such-like and, believe me, that is going to do him no good. What puzzles me most, however, is where he is getting this religion from. It's surely not from us.'

'Now, Mickeen, what harm is it for a boy to talk to God and have a liking for religion? I'd say that you should be proud of him instead of sneaking behind hedges listening to his innocent chats. Anyway, you are forever picking on Sean and beating him for nothing.'

'Look, Bridie, I have to make sure that he gets some sense and doesn't turn out a pure idiot. He won't listen to anything I say. Religion won't feed him, will it?

'Oh indeed, a fat lot you do to feed any of us, let alone Sean. All you think of is drink, night, noon and morning; it's drink with you and to hell with us.'

'That's right, you stick up for the little cur, you only

encourage him. But I'm telling you now that I'll keep beating sense into him. I'll give him school and religion!'

'That's all you're good for, Mickeen, beating women and children. You were never good for anything else except the pub.'

'You're right there, girl, and what's more I'm going to the pub now and to hell with you and them.'

'Go on then, we'll have peace when you're gone, thank God; I only wish that you'd never come back.'

'I might not at that, so watch it. Or maybe you can join Sean and have a chat with your shadow. It should suit you both; the two of you are mad.'

When I heard arguments like this between my parents, I felt for my mother and hated my father. I wanted to get away from them, my father in particular. But the idea or the means for such an escape did not come until I met up with Jimmy Dineen, another travelling boy of about the same age as me.

When my parents were travelling in County Tipperary, they met up with Paddy Dineen, his wife Mary, and their five children. Jimmy, like me, was the eldest and when he and I first met, like all children on the road, we were shy and timid but soon got to know each other. Unlike most of the friendships that I had on the road, my friendship with Jimmy was unique in that it lasted for eight months, whilst both families travelled together.

One day, when Jimmy and I were out mooching, I said to him: 'Jimmy, what will you do when you grow up?'

'I'll get married and get a job maybe,' he said.

'Oh!' said I, taken aback, 'I would not do that, I am going to school and then becoming a priest.'

'I don't think I would ever like to do that,' said Jimmy, 'I suppose it could be all right though. But we wouldn't be together if you became a priest. You would have to stay in a monastery. If we both stayed on the road together we would become very rich dealers.'

'I suppose you're right,' I said, 'but I don't like the road – in fact I hate it.'

'Why? Don't we always have good fun on the road together, especially in the summer?'

'Oh, it can be good in the summer all right, but what about the winter, Jimmy? It's not so good then, is it?'

'Yeah, I suppose you're right, Sean, but I hope you stay on the road; I would hate it if you went away.'

'That's just it, Jimmy, that's just it. You know that any day my parents might move away, and then we might never see each other again. This is why I hate road life – I have so few pals!'

'I see what ya mean, Sean, but I won't be leaving you, because our parents might stay travelling together for years now.'

'I hope so,' I said, 'I pray and hope they do.'

'Hey, Sean, do you pray? I mean really pray?'

'Of course I pray, don't you?'

'Yes, in church I pray a lot,' said Jimmy.

'Wouldn't it be great if the two of us could become priests? We could go all over the world together preaching. Of course we'd have to go to school, but at the moment that's impossible.'

'How is it impossible, Sean? What's to stop us?'

'Oh everything,' I replied, 'First of all, travellers are not allowed to go to school; secondly, our parents would stop us, even if we were allowed, because they would not stay camping in the one place for long. Look, Jimmy, it's getting late and we will be killed if we don't get home fast.'

'Yes, you're right, and to make things worse we didn't mooch much today.'

At the camp our parents were beginning to get worried over our being so late getting home.

'You know, Paddy,' said my father, 'we'll have to separate these two buckos of ours; no matter where one goes, the other goes, and God only knows what devilment they get up to. I'll bet now that the two of them went to the pictures and will come back with one hand as long as the other!'

'When I get my hands on that cur of mine,' said Paddy, 'I'll break his back. I'll give him pictures!'

'Wait! Here they are now,' said my father. 'Well, me young bucks, where have you two been till this hour of the night?'

'Mooching,' I said. 'The pubs were very slack and we waited until they closed in order to get something.'

'Oh, I suppose you did well then, the pair of you? How much did you get?'

'We got about a pound between us, because there was hardly anyone in the helm.'

'Is that what you have been away for all day?' said my father, and grabbed me by the hair, punching and kicking me at the same time. 'You were at the pictures weren't you, you cur?'

'Oh no, Daddy, no,' I roared in pain, as the blood poured from my mouth.

'Get into the tent you cur, before I kill you, and never let me see you and Jimmy Dineen together again, because if I do I'll cripple you, do you hear me?'

'Yes, Daddy, I promise,' I cried, 'please don't beat me any more, please.'

I went to bed and cried through the night with the pain. Jimmy had suffered, too, from his father. The worst, however, was that, for a week or so afterwards, me and Jimmy could not see each other: we were kept separated and closely watched. This for us was the cruellest blow of all.

Ironically, we had both been telling the truth about our reason for being out late.

After the matter had eventually been forgotten, Jimmy and I were together again, back on the road mooching.

'Hey Sean, we're near Cahir now, we've walked the best part of four miles and I'm crolish. I know a good monastery here where we can get a good feed, so let's go there first, before we mooch the helm.'

'Oh I'm game,' I said, 'because I'm peckish too.'

'Now when we get up there, we go to the back jigger, and let me do all the whidding.'

When we reached Cahir we went to the monastery where

a monk took us to a small room and told us to sit whilst he got us something to eat.

About fifteen minutes later the monk brought us both a nice meal of sausages and eggs, tea and bread and butter. Whilst we ate he sat down and began talking to us.

'Well, and where do you two lads hail from, and what's your names?'

'I'm Sean Devine and this is my pal, Jimmy Dineen,' said I, 'we're travellers, Father. I originally came from Mulatty, Father, and Jimmy comes from the county Limerick.'

'I see,' said the monk, 'and do you like travelling around the country?'

'Not really, Father,' I said, 'I would like to be settled down.'

'Me too,' said Jimmy.

'Is that a fact, now?' asked the monk. 'I would have thought that you liked travelling the road, what with no school to worry about and without a care in the world. Sure it is a grand life you have.'

'That's the funny thing, Father,' I said, 'everyone thinks it's great being on the road, but it's not really. I hate it!'

'Me too,' said Jimmy.

'Well, is that a fact, now?' said the monk, 'I didn't know that now. Well, could you tell me why you don't like the road?'

'I don't know, really, Father, but I would like to live in a house and be able to go to school,' I said. 'Jimmy here would like that too, Father, because we are good pals and we would like to go to school together.'

'I think you boys are pulling my leg now,' said the monk. 'School how are you? You haven't a notion of going to school!'

'Oh I have, Father,' I said, 'honest I have, but the only thing is that we can't go to school because we travel all the time. That is why I would like to be living in a house.'

'Now, tell me another thing,' said the monk, 'what would you be wanting school for anyway? Sure when you both grow up you'll get married, and more than likely will want to stay on the road. Do you both ever think about this?'

'We don't have to, Father,' I said quickly, 'or at least I don't have to, because I am going to be a priest like you when I grow up.'

'God bless your innocent faith child, but you must remember that it is hard being a priest. But tell me now, what put this idea in your head?'

'Well, when I was small,' I said, 'a nun told me all about St Francis and about a whole lot of other holy priests who died for their faith and love of God. That's why I want to be a priest too, so that I can die for my faith.'

'Nowadays priests rarely die for their faith like they did in the past. Those were in the bad days when people did not want to believe in God. But today everyone knows about God, so there is no need for people to die for their faith.'

'I don't care,' I said, 'I still want to be a priest, because I want to work for God.'

'Yes, Father, Sean is right,' said Jimmy. 'I want to be a priest too, but what I'd like to know is this: could me and Sean become priests? I mean, us being travellers and all that. Sean thinks that because we are travellers we could not become priests. Is that right, Father?'

'Of course not, child, anyone can become a priest. But it takes a very long time, for school and study. You just can't become a priest straight away. One day, if you both pray especially to God, you may become priests; if God wants you to be priests it rests with his will. So you must both pray very hard to Jesus and his Blessed Mother for the grace to become priests. God is slow but sure in his divine way, so always remember too that I will say a special prayer that God will make you all he wants you to be.

'Well children, I have to leave you now for I must attend my prayers and I shall pray for you both; but you must pray for me too, and if you do I know that almighty God and his Blessed Mother will eventually help us, so mind yourselves; and I have got a parcel of food, so you can take it home to your families.'

'Thank you, Father,' I said, 'I shall pray all the time and I won't forget you.'

'I won't either,' said Jimmy, 'and thank you.'

'That's all right boys, and God bless you both and also your families. I hope, by the will of God, that your every wish comes true.'

We left the monastery very enlightened and quite happy.

'Here, Jimmy, we'd better do a bit of mooching, it's getting late and we have no grade yet,' said I, as we went.

'All right, we'll do the pubs, Sean, but watch out for the shades.'

Jimmy and I went into a pub where we began begging. When left alone by the landlord, we sang a song and then went around collecting; and on this particular night, in Cahir, after having been to most of the pubs, we earned about eight pounds between us, a good night's taking.

'Well here's the two boyos,' said my mother, when we arrived back at the camp. 'Well, Sean, how did you get on tonight?'

'We got choicer,' I said, 'the town was very bad.'

'I'll give you choicer,' said my mother, 'if you try kidding me. Sure can't I see the parcel under your arm and the smile on your kisser, and on Jimmy's too?'

'No, Mammy, we done very well, we got four lunters each and a parcel of food at the monastery,' I said.

'You're great lads, indeed,' said my mother. 'What would we do without them, Mrs Dineen?'

'Oh, they are topping little moochers,' said Mrs Dineen. 'Come and sit down, creatures, you both must be fagged out, and get some supper, goodness knows but you've earned it.'

'That's right, boys,' said my mother, 'sit down and I'll get your supper ready. Did you see your fathers when you were in town?'

'Yes,' I said, 'they're pretty drunk too; they wanted money off us but we would not give them any.'

'Quite right, too,' said my mother, 'let them beg their own money for their drink.'

There was VIP treatment for us that night, but only because we had earned the money. If, however, we had earned only a little money, the welcome to supper would have been non-existent. Such are the ups and downs for children of the road in their daily lives. After supper that night, when the younger children were in bed, myself and my pal Jimmy sat up by the fire with our mothers, waiting for our fathers to come home from their drinking session. Whilst we sat by the fireside, we told our mothers about the monk we had talked to earlier that day.

'Some – indeed all – of those poor monks are very good,' said my mother. 'They don't be allowed to carry money, though, because they have to take a vow of poverty; that's why they don't even wear socks. Bless them, they live a very hard life too in them monasteries. They have to get up at cock crow and do hard work and prayer all day. They are very holy men, God bless them.

'Irish monks have a great history; there are hundreds of holy places in Ireland where they lived and died hundreds of years ago. Places such as Glendalough, Clonmacnoise, Kildare, Kerry, Athenry, Cashel and many more. The strange thing about the Irish monks of long ago is that the most of them were travelling people who had become monks through the influence of St Patrick, himself a great lover of the travelling people. Take St Kevin, now, who stayed most of his life in Glendalough; he started off living in a little tent and slowly, with the help of some travellers, he built a church. Musha God help him, he built it very simple; for in those days they hadn't the tools or cement we have now.

'In those times too, most of the people in Ireland were pagan and warlike. The people used to live in clans and were always fighting. At first poor St Kevin did not know what to do in order to spread the Word of God around Ireland; he was getting very old himself and could not get around like he used to.

'Then he had a vision, and in that vision he was told to teach some families of travellers who were camping not so far away. So off went St Kevin to the travellers, and within a few days they knew every word of the Gospel. St Kevin himself was amazed by their quickness in learning and could only thank God for his goodness. St Kevin then told the people that, as travellers who journeyed the length and breadth of the country or, if not, meeting other travellers who did, they were to preach the word of God throughout Ireland.

'And because of that little bunch of travellers, many, many great and holy monks walked the roads of Ireland, Scotland, England and Wales, and many other foreign and far-off shores, spreading the Gospel of God.

'Now,' continued my mother, 'before St Kevin died, in his little camping ground in Glendalough, he got twenty or thirty travelling families around by the side of one of the lakes and gave them a sermon. The words of this sermon were passed down by word of mouth from generation to generation of travellers.

'It wasn't a very long sermon, but it was one that will never be forgotten by travellers, as long as the world shall last. Now the gist of the sermon is this: St Kevin said: "My brothers and my sisters, God has been very good to us, his lowly brethren; we beg our bit of food or we fashion little earthen jars, so that the sons, relations and friends of our four feuding kings may dine and drink. We fashion the beads and bangles that adorn their earthly bodies. We fashion and hone the wattles that sometimes strengthen their forts, and we do all this in beggary. But now we have fashioned the greatest gift from God to man, the Divine Word of God. My brothers and sisters, in my vision I saw many dark and unholy deeds in the future generations, but reaming steadfast throughout it all will be the Gospel of God which was first preached by us and our holy forebears. In that vision I saw king fighting king, nation fighting nation, and through it all the travelling people were treated as outcast, nay as dogs who eat their own vomit. But even through this great degradation, humiliation, hate and persecution, the travelling people keep their great faith in

Almighty God. In the vision I see them becoming a race of people apart, no longer the heralds of God, but instead humiliated and outcast beings. Though they'll no longer be the heralds of God's Word, they shall have a faith and love in God that none other shall equal. Though the earthly world shall harass and degrade them, Almighty God shall bless them twofold. The time shall come too, brothers and sisters, when the travelling people of Ireland shall be no more. When this day comes, the guilty will reach and tear the hearts of the landed gentry. The world shall know of the goodness that was the travelling people of Ireland. Ireland, or the hard-hearted people of Ireland, shall mourn the passing of the most unique race of people in the world. God, however, in his infinite wisdom, will give by the loss to the world of his beloved travellers, an example that will renew faith in man. For, as the world mourns the loss of so unique a race of people as the travellers of Ireland, so also will they examine themselves, and through this great loss the world will be renewed in faith and love of Almighty God. This, brethren, is the vision. Now I must go to my Divine Maker, for troubled and weary of heart am I for each and every one of you, my brothers and sisters."

'After this,' my mother continued, 'St Kevin lay down on his bed of stone and passed from this world to meet his Maker.'

'Mammy,' I asked, when the tale was ended, 'how do you know about St Kevin? Did it really happen like you said?'

'Of course it did, Sean; for years upon years now travellers have gone to the patterns around Ireland, to those such as Athenry, Lough Derg, Clonmacnoise and many more. They go to these places because they hold special meaning for the travellers. Of course we used to beg at these patterns, but prayer was our aim too.'

Later she told us another story about a blessed well in a large tree.

'You see,' she said, 'not far from Mountrath, on the Portlaoise side, there is a large old tree, and high up in this tree there is a little hollow, and in it there is a little well. At least, the hollow of the tree has water in it. It looks just like a little wooden bowl full of water. Now this tree with its well has a very strange history and for years the travellers used to hold a pattern there; of course you know that, nowadays, all these patterns are dying out.

'Well, anyway,' my mother continued, 'many, many years ago, in a field not far away from the tree, was a Blessed Well, known as 'Colaney Well', and it was used hundreds of years ago by priests who had to hide because they were being persecuted and killed for the Faith. They could not say Mass in public, so they had to find secret places to say it. Now the Colaney Well marks the spot where one poor priest used to say Mass for his little crowd of followers. They had to say the Mass in secret and always be on the look-out for the soldiers who were their persecutors. Anyway, children, this poor priest and his followers did not escape the tyrants' hands. As the priest was saying Mass for his little band of twenty or thirty poor souls – and among them were many travellers, bless them – the priest and his little congregation were murdered in cold blood by a band of soldiers. The priest, God bless him, was tortured before his body was cut to pieces.

'This, however, was not to be the end of the tragedy; there was to be another murder of yet another priest many years after the first. This came through the pattern that used to take place each year in memory of the martyrdom of the priest and his followers. At times there used be very large crowds at this pattern; they came with the priests who said Mass in the open and offered up prayers to the martyrs. Anyway, this went on for years and years, the pattern getting larger as the years went by. Then, two hundred years or so ago, troubles began in Ireland again, the '98 troubles they were called; this time two people were murdered, a priest and one of his helpers.

'This priest and his helper lived nearby, and nearly every day they went to the well to pray, as well as to tend and care for it. On one such mission the two were murdered, and this foul murder went unnoticed for many years because of the great trouble and turmoil that was in Ireland at the time. Anyway, the troubles ended and religious freedom once again returned to Ireland – that is to say, people could go to Mass again and not be persecuted.

'When peace had returned, strange things began to happen near the site of Colaney Well, which goes to show that the wonder of God never ceases. It began very simply indeed, when a travelling family pulled in to camp for the night, on the side of the road. The family consisted of a husband and wife and five or six young children. They built their camp under a large tree, lit a fire, ate their supper, and went to bed. It was an autumn night, just like any other to the travelling family; little indeed did they know what a strange night was to be in store for them.

'Well,' continued my mother, 'they went to bed and had been there but a few hours when the happenings of that night began. A loud cooing noise, like the sound of a woodpigeon, awakened the travelling man and his wife. They did not pay much heed to the cooing at first; they assumed it to be pigeons roosting up in the tree over their heads.

'After half an hour or so, however, they both were irritated by the continuous cooing sound because they could not get back to sleep. They were also afraid that the noise might waken the youngest children, who were very cross at the best of times. The husband, not able to stand it any longer, decided to get up and throw something at the tree to frighten the birds; this he duly did.

'However, as he threw a bit of stick up into the tree, he saw a very bright glow. At first he thought it was someone sitting up in the tree with a torch trying to scare him; but no; very gradually, the figures of two snow-white doves appeared in the tree. What stunned the travelling man most was the beautiful glow that was coming from them. They shone like the sun, and the cooing sound they made was like beautiful music to the ear. After a bit the poor man got over the initial shock, and he became entranced by the beauty of the birds he was seeing and hearing.

'The travelling man called his wife without taking his eyes off the shining doves – for doves they were, shining whiter than any snow. His wife came out of the tent and she too became entranced by the beauty they saw. About a half hour or so later the two doves flew out of the tree and, still glowing white against the darkness of the sky, lighted on a stone in the field a mere hundred yards or so away. A short time later, whilst the man and woman still watched, in mute wonderment, the beauty before their eyes, the two doves, still shining and cooing, flew back to the tree-branch where they were first seen. As the doves sat on the branch, rays of light, like rays of sunlight, came down on them through the leaves of the tree. The man and woman were amazed at the sight before their eyes, and the more so because they could not understand the meaning of such beauty. Then, through the rays of light that shone on the doves, the man and woman saw small, shining, shimmering crystals fall, like rain, onto the doves, and then gather in a cluster in the fork of the tree. Suddenly a voice, the likes of which the travellers never heard before, spoke: "Be not afraid, for what you see is not crystals, but water from the blood of men and priests who died for the love of their Redeemer. This blood, now turned to water, shall remain in this tree until the end of time, for mortal man shall ne'er destroy it. It shall be, for you and yours, who travel the weary road, a place of pilgrimage."

'The beautiful-sounding voice stopped; the travelling man and woman, completely awed by what was happening that night, gazed up at the shining doves, still speechless but feeling radiantly happy. Suddenly, the doves left the tree and began flying heavenwards, their heavenly glow getting darker and darker as they flew higher and higher, until eventually they were no more. The man and woman did not speak but returned to their tent, where they both, with all their children, slept in eternal sleep.

'Well, children,' continued my mother, 'the very next day the travelling man, his wife and children were all found dead in bed. It was only through the years shortly after their death that the whole story came out. It was told to many travellers, by the spirit of the dead man, whenever they camped for a night under the tree. So you see, children,' said my mother, 'that is why travellers still pay a visit to Colaney Well, which is now up in the tree. Now, there is still one strange thing about this well in the tree, and it's this; no matter how you try to empty this well, either with a mug – that is – dip it into the well and fill it and then throw the water away, the water in the well still remains full to the rim of the well; even if you spent all day emptying the water out of it, it would stay full to the brim. Of course a lot of people will say that there is a spring going up the trunk of the tree, like a tap or something, and that's why it stays full, but if this was the case the well would overflow; it never overflows nor goes dry, no matter how wet the weather or how warm. The well always remains full, no more and no less. Even to this very day you can see this well in the tree near Mountrath. On the tree, too, you will see little bits of cloth, medals and beads left there over the years by many travellers as a sort of offering to the goodness of God and the sacredness of the place. So there you are, children,' said my mother, 'that's the true story of Colaney Well.'

6

A country postman could hardly do his job without the use of a bicycle. Yet his dependence on a bike was nothing in comparison with the pavvy's need of a horse. Like the bike, little attention was paid to the horse as long as he was in working order. He was fed more often out of necessity than out of love. Sometimes he was turned loose in a field or on the long mile and expected to forage for himself.

Now and then my father, in one of his rarer moments, would get up and scour the neighbourhood for a bit of hay for the horse. He did just that one evening in late autumn after we had made a camp outside Mitchelstown in County Cork.

'Bridie,' he said before he left, 'I'm going to look for a bundle of hay for the old pragg. I won't be long, so have a sup of tea ready by the time I'm back. I'll be no more that ten minutes.'

True to his word, my father was soon back, but instead of hay he brought a bag of beet pulp. When he got back to the camp he said to Mammy, 'Bridie, woman, we're in luck, I have a right feed here for the oul' horse. I collered it in a sark up the road. Would you believe it, there's plenty more there in a large trough. There's cattle and sheep feeding on it in a field; I'm to go back and get three or four bags because it will last a good while.

'Hey Sean,' he shouted, 'you get an old bag and come with me this time; we'll make two trips and that will be enough. We must try to slip into the field and out again without being seen.'

An hour or so later my father had put four bags of beet pulp into the cart, under the cover, to be kept for the horse. He gave him half a bagful to eat meanwhile.

'Gosh, Bridie,' he said, delighted, 'that's great stuff, that beet pulp. I have just given the old horse half a bagful and he's devouring it. That stuff will put great condition on him for the winter.'

'He needs a bit of conditioning,' said my mother, 'because at the moment he is only skin and bones.'

'Well he won't be skin and bones when he gets that pulp down him, I can guarantee you that.'

Everything was dandy that night for my father and his horse, but the following morning he was to get quite a shock. After breakfast he told my mother that he was going for the horse to give him another bit of pulp, but about ten minutes later he came running back up the road.

'Bridie, do you hear me? The horse is croaked.'

'What do you mean, croaked?' asked my mother.

'What I said woman! What I said – stark, stone dead by the side of the road – how, I don't know. I'll have to go and tell the guards to get it moved, otherwise we'll get a summons.'

Later, when a local guard came on the scene and looked at the dead horse, he said to my father, 'I'm afraid your horse has choked himself. What did you give him to eat?'

'Oh, I just gave him a half bag of beet pulp,' said my father.

'Dry beet pulp?' asked the guard.

'Yes, that's right,' said my father.

'Well, me good man, when you gave him that pulp, in its dry form, you killed your own horse.'

'Well, that couldn't be, Guard, because I seen cattle and sheep eating it and it didn't harm them,' said my father.

'True,' said the guard, 'it doesn't affect them because they have a double stomach, but with a horse it's different because he can't bring it up to chew, like a cow can. If you had soaked the pulp for twenty-four hours it would have been safe. You see, you gave your horse dry beet pulp and as it got damp in his windpipe it expanded and choked him. Don't worry though, I'll get the carcass removed, and maybe our local welfare people will be able to give you something to buy another animal. At any rate I will have a word with the welfare officer for you.'

'Thanks very much, Guard,' said my father, 'thanks very much. It's very good of you.'

When he got back to the camp, he told my mother the whole story. When she heard it she burst out laughing.

'What's funny, woman? Are you in your humour or what?'

'I'm laughing at you, you poor gomey,' said my mother. 'Good conditioner for the horse my eye. It was good all right, it made him fit to choke himself. And to make sure, you weren't satisfied with one bag, you had to get five. Great stuff? I'll say it was! It was so good that the old horse never got over it.' My father, even though the circumstances were far from funny, had to join Mammy in laughter over the incident. Indeed, it became a funny topic around many a camp-fire for years afterwards. However, everything worked out well, for a week or so later my father got another horse with the help of the Welfare Authority.

Shortly after this incident, my family and the Dineens met up with Tearaway Sweeney and his wife Meggy McGegg. Tearaway and Meggy had three sons and all three were foolish in their way of going through life. The funniest thing about the Sweeney family was that they all had nicknames, and to hear them at each other with these names was always funny. The three sons were Tom the Mog, who was about twenty years old, Humpy Joe who was seventeen, and Seldom Fed who was fourteen. The whole family were a bit simple and great fun to be living with. With the Sweeneys there was never a dull moment.

Jimmy and I loved the Mog, Humpy and Seldom Fed, and great indeed was the fun we had together, especially when all five of us went on a begging expedition. The first night after meeting, both families gathered round the one big fire, all pooling their resources for one big meal between all. After the meal began story and talking time around the roaring fire.

My father started the ball rolling by asking Tearaway how he got his name.

'Well you see, like when Tearaway talks, or at least asks others to talk, he always says "Tearaway with your tale",' said his wife.

'And she,' said Tearaway, 'gets her name because she looks like an ould goat, hence Meggy McGegg. My eldest son is called Mog, Humpy goes around in a daze, as if he had a load on his back, and Seldom Fed is never done eating. So between McGegg, the Mog, Humpy and Seldom, I'd need to be a Tearaway. And do you know that the four of them are pure idiots.'

'That'll do you now, Tearaway, that'll do you,' said Meggy. 'Sure you haven't a notion of what you are saying now, have you?'

'Whisht your mouth, nanny-goat, you're talking in circles, you are, with your goateen's face on you. You know, Mickeen,' he said to my father, 'that woman talks backwards sometimes and she has me as bad as herself, she has.'

'Ah, I don't know about that,' said my father, 'I think it's a grand family you make, a grand family, God bless you all! And besides, it makes no difference how you talk now, so long as you can mooch.'

'Bedad, you're sound there, Mickeen, you're sound,' mimicked Meggy, 'that's more than I can say for you, you Tearaway, you.'

'Lookit here, goat face, if I want a parrot, I can buy one who will mimic me better than you can, so put that in your whiskers and snuff it, you ould hag you.'

'Hey you,' interrupted the Mog, 'don't you be calling my Mammy a hag, that's not nice.'

'Well listen, me big fool,' said Tearaway, 'if I want anyone's opinion it won't be a gom's, so keep yours for yourself. Goodness knows but you need them for your brothers.'

'Mammy,' said the Mog, 'Daddy is calling me a gom.'

'Sure you are a gom,' replied his mother, 'and you still don't know it. It's a terrible thing to be a fool, but it's far worse being a fool and not knowing it.'

'Ah, you're as bad as him, one minute you are fighting

him, the next you're taking his part,' said the Mog, 'all you do is call me a gom all the time.'

'Sure you are a gom,' said his mother. 'I'm tired telling you that. Indeed, between the three of ye, I'm well yoked with fools, God bless us, indeed I am.'

Thus lamented Meggy about her family, a family who were forever running each other down, and all the time one was every bit as bad as the other.

I liked the Sweeney family, for to me they were a great source of fun. I liked Meggy best of all though, especially since the night I heard her tell the story of how the mogs, her sons, got involved with cats in a graveyard. I was sitting by the fire with all the others the night Meggy told it.

'Musha,' began Meggy, 'I'll never forget that night for years to come. It began on the road between Littleton and Horse and Jockey, not far from Cashel. Well, at the time we were camping near the village of Horse and Jockey. The three boyoes went to Cashel earlier that evening to do the chats. They got a lift in to Cashel somehow, foolish and all as they are, but they had to walk home. The journey was ten or twelve miles I think, anyway it was around eleven at night when they started out for home.

'Well,' Meggy continued, 'everything went fine with the boyos until they came to the graveyard. You all probably know the place well. It's only a mile or so outside the village.'

'Anyway, to continue,' said Meggy, 'we waited up until about midnight for them to return, but no sign, so we went to bed, not too worried, for we guessed that they had had to walk and wouldn't be here for hours.

'The following morning I went out to look in their tent to see if they were there, but found it empty. "That's unusual," I said to Tearaway, "they're never out like this, there must be something wrong. Maybe they're lying dead by the roadside, after being knocked down by a car or something." "Arrah whisht, woman, they're not so foolish as to walk under a car," Tearaway said.

'Well,' said Meggy, 'the heart was up in me mouth with worry. All kinds of things went through my mind and, without any more ado, I made Tearaway yoke the old ass under the cart and off the two of us headed for Cashel.

'About a mile or two beyond the graveyard we found the three fools sitting down by the side of the main road, with big silly grins on their foolish faces, God bless the mark. Well I needn't tell you I gave them a bit of a telling off. Then they told us what happened them on their way home from the chats. Better still, Humpy here will tell you everything himself. Go on Humpy, tell everyone about the pussies.'

'Oh, all right, Mammy,' said Humpy as he began. 'Well we was walking because not one person would stop to give us a lift, and I can tell you it was all the work of the devil. It was a very bright night because the moon was full and there wasn't a cloud in the sky. Me, the Mog and Seldom Fed were talking about the picture we had seen in Cashel as we walked the road home.

'All went fine until we were nearly opposite the gate of the cemetery, then things began to happen. First of all, we heard voices, men's voices, coming from the cemetery. All three of us stopped in our tracks and looked into the graveyard. What we saw was indeed the work of the devil. First of all there was one big black cat nearly as big as a donkey sitting on its hind legs on one of the tombstones. Around him sat about ten or twelve other cats. The one on the stone was talking to the rest; after a bit they all started to sing like drunken men. The boyo on the tombstone hunched his back, raised himself on his hind legs and, with eyes shining like live coals, began to dance a kind of dance whilst the others screamed like demons. Well, I felt the cold sweat dripping down my face. I felt my hair standing on edge. Seldom Fed and the Mog were galloping like the hammers of hell. I tried to follow, but at first I couldn't move a muscle with fright. I felt as if I was glued to the ground. Anyway, when I heard the black bucko dancing on the tombstone shouting out "Get him quick!" I soon started to shift. I don't really know how fast I went but I know that though my brothers had a good start on me, I overtook them within a matter of seconds. We eventually sat down by the roadside, exhausted. There we stayed for the rest of the night, afraid to go any further either way. But though we were about a mile away from the cemetery, we could hear the devil cats howling and singing until daylight.'

'There you are now,' said Meggy, taking up the story, 'there's my three gombeens for you, afraid of a few old tom-cats having a night out. Dancing indeed! Whoever heard of cats dancing, especially on tombstones? Do you know what went wrong that night? It was the pictures. The pictures made them imagine these things. Singing cats!'

Yes, I could easily like such characters as the Sweeney lads. It was not often that I had such company on the road. It was a life of 'here today, gone tomorrow'. Shortly after our stay with the Sweeneys we were off on our travels again.

We didn't travel too long on our own, however. Once more we met the Dineen family and travelled with them for two months. Naturally Jimmy Dineen and myself were delighted to be together again. During this latter two months we became even greater pals and when our parents parted, after two months travelling together, it was to affect me very deeply. We were eating our supper when we overheard them discussing moving to different counties for the following winter. When we heard them, we both quietly left the fireside and went up the road out of sight and sound and talked about the break-up.

'Jimmy,' I said, 'I wish our parents wouldn't move, it doesn't seem right. That is the best of living in a house, they couldn't pack up and move. I always say that God isn't fair. He could stop this if he liked, but he doesn't, why?'

'Oh, I don't think you should blame God, Sean,' said Jimmy. 'After all, we might meet again very soon like the last time.'

'That's just it, Jimmy,' I cried, 'it's always put aside as not being long, but it is long, and lonely too. I always feel this loneliness. I always wish that I could live in a house or some place where I would not feel lonely. Even when I go to the pictures they make me sad and lonelier.'

'But that couldn't be,' interrupted Jimmy, 'I always enjoy watching a good film. I'd never feel lonely in a picture hall.'

'I do, though,' I affirmed. 'You see, if I am at a picture with you I don't feel lonely, but when I go on my own I envy, in a way, the other kids around me chatting and laughing with each other.'

'But you are wrong to think like this, Sean,' said Jimmy. 'Who knows, but one day you will have a home like settled people, and so will I. I promise you that when I get bigger I will leave my parents and come with you. The two of us will get on real well then.'

'It would not be bad I suppose for us to be together, but I keep thinking what we could do. I don't think we could go to school on our own. No one would let us.'

'That's where you're wrong, Sean,' said Jimmy. 'When we are big no one can stop us.'

On the following day, on the camping road outside the town of Thurles, I sat sobbing my heart out as I watched my pal move away with his family, hoping against hope that he would soon return. Little did I know that we were never to meet again. The departure had been too much. Over the following few days I sat brooding all the time.

Then things began to happen which changed my whole outlook. It all began very simply. I was asked to go for a can of water one night. We were camping at the time near Templemore and the little well was just a quarter of a mile or so from the camp. I was just dipping the can into the well when the thought of running away leaped into my mind.

'That's it,' I said to myself, 'I'll run away and go back towards Thurles to find Jimmy, I'll bet they are camping the far side of Thurles, or else near the railway bridge outside Tipperary town. I'll leave the can here near the well, so that my little brother Mickeeny or some of the others can find it. Why didn't I think of this sooner? I should have done it long ago. I bet my father will be sorry when he finds out I'm gone. I'll be glad.'

I started the journey to Thurles. I walked the best part of

six miles in nearly as many hours. Then, tired, I sat down by the roadside and slept for an hour or so. After the rest, I got up and resumed my journey, arriving at the camping ground outside Thurles at about six o'clock in the morning. When I arrived at the place my heart sank, for the road was deserted. No Jimmy. Suddenly I fully realised that I was really alone. I sat by the roadside and burst into tears, as I muttered to myself. 'What am I to do now? If I go on to Tipperary then Jimmy might not be there either. I can't go back home because Daddy would kill me. What, in the name of God, can I do? Or why on earth did I do it at all?'

These were the questions that were running through my mind. I sat by the roadside for hours crying over my plight. Eventually I went into Thurles where I got a meal at the convent in the main street. After that I headed for Tipperary, thumbing a lift for most of the way.

When I got to the camping ground near Tipperary I was in for another shock, for that place too was deserted. This brought on another fit of crying and a feeling of complete desolation. Now I felt lonelier than ever in my life before. I missed my mother and little brothers and sisters, even my father, but I knew in my heart that I could not go back to them on account of what my father would do to me.

'Where can I go?' I asked myself, 'Oh, dear God, help me!' After many hours I decided that I would head for Dara, my father's home town. I knew I had several relations there and this thought inspired me to go there.

'If I go to Dara,' I thought, 'I can stay with Aunt Mary or Uncle Paddy. I could live in their house and go to school.'

I started walking the main road. Shortly, however, I got a lift in a car to Newbridge. When I got there, I was told that Dara was still a good bit away yet. I then went to the convent and got a good meal. After this I begged a few of the houses and when I got enough money I decided to go to the pictures in Newbridge, after which I would go into some old hayshed and sleep for the night and on to Dara the following morning.

Meanwhile, back in Templemore, some fifty or sixty miles from Newbridge, my family was very worried. When I didn't come back an hour or so after being sent for the water, my mother became very anxious.

'Mickeen,' she said to my father, 'will you go and see what's keeping Sean. I feel sure something has happened to him. He wouldn't be this late coming back with a drop of water.'

'Can't you stop worrying, woman? Don't you know well that fellow mopes along. If it'll satisfy you, I'll go in a few minutes.'

'Can't you go now, Mickeen, I told you that there is something after happening to him. Don't you ask me how I know. I just know it, that's all.'

'Okay, I'll go now, and when I get my hands on him I'll kill him,' said my father.

He went to the well and when he got there he lit some matches for it was pitch dark. He found the can of water near the well where I had left it, and immediately panicked; fearing the worst, he looked into the well. In so doing he wasted nearly all his matches. My father knew the well was very deep and somehow or other he felt that I was at the bottom.

'I must go to the guards,' he said to himself. 'I must get help. If Bridie finds out it will kill her. I wish to God I had went for that water myself.'

My father then ran to town as fast as he could and told the guards. Shortly afterwards a few guards, with my father, hurried to the well with ropes and a grappling iron. With a large torch they searched the well which was very clean; they could see the bottom. After groping around with the iron they knew that, whatever had happened to me, I had not fallen into the well.

Within a short space of time, however, there was a nationwide search for me. My mother, on hearing of my disappearance, had to be taken to hospital suffering from severe shock.

For weeks, even months, there was no trace of me despite a nationwide appeal in the press and on the radio.

The ground seemed to have opened up and swallowed me. As the months passed, my mother became a nervous wreck. On five or six occasions she had to be removed to hospital where she underwent deep sedation; even my father, for the first time in many years, completely gave up drinking. He had given up hope of ever finding me again and now he was afraid that he was going to lose his wife too, through her worrying. Even the other travellers he met tried to console him. They would all say very much the same. 'I'm very sorry for your trouble, Mickeen, but God is good, your son will be all right.'

'I feel that, too,' said my father, 'but what I can't get over is that there is no word to say whether he is alive or dead. Why on earth does God allow this to happen to us? There's my poor wife worrying herself to death over Sean, and goodness knows I haven't had much sleep myself since he left. If only he was well and alive I'd be happy, but it's not knowing how he is that's really killing me.'

'Please God,' the others would say, 'he will turn up safe and sound, have no fear.'

My father, however, was to remain worrying, as was mother, for many many months. Day in and day out was spent in the hope of getting some word about me, but in vain.

'You know, Bridie,' said my father one night, as he sat by the fire with her, 'we are an unlucky family; why, I don't really know. Ever since he sat up laughing all night in that old lane near Thurles, I am convinced there is something unusual about him.'

'Don't be daft, man,' said my mother, 'there's nothing wrong with the poor lost creature. You always hated him and that's the reason he's missing. You drove him away and you know in your heart you did.'

'I did no such thing as drive him away, this was his own doing and I keep telling you that there is something funny about Sean.'

99

7

I often wonder myself if there was something a bit unusual about me, for around this period my mind was too active. I wanted to learn all the time; I thirsted to know more and still more of the world around me. Then I met the most remarkable man I have ever met in my life. He was old, but while normally the young resent the advice of the aged, he had a great influence over me. I would say that whatever learning I got in the years afterwards, none was greater than what I learned listening to the old man in Kilkenny those many years ago.

I discovered that Shakespeare was a traveller for most of his early years, picking and learning legends from travellers whom he met. Even Chaucer travelled in pilgrimage to complete his tales of the foot-sloggers who went to Canterbury, most of whom were itinerant tradesmen. Bunyan, I learnt, was the son of a humble tinsmith.

I learned that these men did not need a great or 'grand' education to relate their classics but, instead, a deep and profound love and understanding of humankind and the wonder of the world around them. Nearly all the great figures of literature gathered their experience through their wanderings. They learned to write as easily and as simply as the night turns to day. This I learned from a humble doll-man at the end of his wanderings.

The people of the road have a unique culture, which has been passed down through generations of travelling people in Ireland. It has always fascinated me from the time when, on my mother's knee, I first heard the tales of the travelling people. As I grew, so did my fascination, until it embraced every aspect of our culture. Others took it for granted. I thought a lot about it. I wanted answers and reasons for everything.

One night, shortly after leaving home, I came across the camp of two old people on the side of the golflinks road outside Kilkenny. I had seen the old man and his wife working the town during the day. The man had a little hand-cart affair, with a flat table-like top. On it an ornately-dressed puppet danced while he pulled the strings. He had some form of music box in the cart and this required winding every so often. The doll-man attracted a large audience of townspeople and children, and from his expression you would imagine that he danced his doll solely to amuse them. His wife slipped, unnoticed, in and out of the crowd with the knobbing bag, collecting.

That night I got talking to the doll-man. He, seeing me look the worse for wear, invited me to his camp, a two-wheeled barrel-topped caravan known to travellers as a 'commodation'. 'You can stay here with me and Nelly, if you like,' said the doll-man. I hesitated.

'What's the matter?' says he, 'Are your parents near here?'

'Oh, my parents are a long way away,' I lied, 'I came here to see an uncle of mine, but I couldn't find him so I'm on my way home again. My parents are staying near Tipperary. I won't have far to go.'

'Well, that's all right, son. What's your name, anyway?' asked the doll-man.

'Sean Devine,' I answered.

'You're not Mickeen's son, are you?'

'Yes,' I said.

'Well, fancy that now,' said the doll-man, 'I know your parents very well, son. You know them too, Nelly, don't you?'

'Well, I declare,' said Nelly, 'why of course I know poor Bridie and Mickeen. Mind you, the children were very small when we last seen them, but now I do see the likeness of Mickeen in his son here.'

'Yes, Nelly, he's a real Mickeen and no mistake. Well, get on a good feed for the lad and make down a good bed for him on the floor. Whilst you are doing that, us men will talk about old times. Musha, God be with the days your father and I spent together back in Clare.'

'I have often heard him speak about you,' I said. 'My daddy used to say that the dancing-doll man was the best company you could have on the road; he said you were a great man for the stories.'

'Is that a fact now? Still the same old Mickeen – does he still drink, though?' asked the doll-man.

'Yes,' I said, 'he still drinks. That's the trouble, he drinks and drinks and drin....'

'Here now, son, what's this crying for? There's no need to cry,' said the doll-man. 'What is really wrong, son? You haven't told me the truth, have you?'

'Oh, leave the poor lad be,' said Nelly. 'Come, son, everything will be all right. Don't you worry; we'll look after you, so there's no need to cry. Here, have this bit to eat now, and then you'll feel better and we'll have a nice talk, won't that be good?'

'Oh yes,' I said. It's just that I felt so lonely when you mentioned my parents and I must tell....'

'Nonsense!' said Nelly. 'You get something to eat first and then we can talk about everything.'

'That's right, son,' said the doll-man. 'You get stuck into the chuck first and we can whid later.'

I ate a hearty supper and felt comfortable for the first time for many a day. The old man talked of life in a way I had never heard before. Sitting around a good fire in the stove, he began: 'Well, Sean, me lad, how do you feel now after your supper?'

'Oh, I feel grand thanks,' I said.

'Good,' the doll-man said, 'now you might tell us what you are really doing on your own.'

'Well,' I said, 'I ran away to try and get to school. I don't like the road.'

'Is that all then?' said the old man. 'You don't like the road, so you ups and walks out, but by it all you are on the road *now*, in a worse state, alone and shelterless. Oh goodness me, the folly of innocent boyhood! Listen, son, have you thought about your parents worrying their hearts out over you?'

'Yes, I know that Mammy will worry a lot,' I said, 'but I know that I'd never be happy at home.'

'Son,' said the old man, 'you would be far happier at home than roaming the road on your own. In life you can't have continuous happiness, you meet many sorrows as well as joys. To face both takes a man, so you too should learn to take them like a man.'

'I know this,' I said, 'but it doesn't seem fair, we are always mocked and hunted by the gentry people. As well as this, there is always drinking and fighting going on on the road. It wouldn't be too bad if Daddy stopped his drinking.'

'Well, son,' said the old man, 'I'll have to grant you that. If your father could stop drinking he would be a millionaire. Time was when I travelled with your dad through Clare; through such places as Ennis, Ennistymon, Whitegate and Corofin. During that time your dad took the pledge and within weeks we had earned between us nigh on half a thousand quid, which was a lot of money in those days. Yes, your father could have been a very wealthy man but for his drink. But this is all the more why you should like him and stick by him and not run away like an idiot.'

'But I do like my father,' said I, 'it's the drink I don't like and the way people mock and jeer us.'

'People mock and jeer? Well, I suppose there's some sense in what you say. The country is indeed a strange place towards what it was in yester year.'

'Did they mock and jeer you when you were small?' I asked.

'They did and they didn't, if you get what I mean. There is, however, one thing I do know; the road will never be the same as it was in the days when I was a lad like you.'

'Could you tell us about the days when you were small?' I asked.

"Musha, son, I will, but a fat lot of good it'll do you. You see, I am nearly seventy-six years of age and have been on the road for every day of it, as was my father, and my grandfather and great-great grandfather, God rest them.

'When I was a lad on the road times were hard, what with the First World War and the Troubles in this country, but nevertheless we travellers were useful then. We were able to do a service for the country, like making and mending pots and pans, doing carpentry, ironwork and various other skills. Even those on the road who had no trade, and these were very few, were able to be of service to the community. They could buy and sell articles that were useful. In those days there was not the supply of cars or lorries as now. Therefore those living right out in the country were glad to see the traveller coming to their door to sell his wares.

'Then, of course, the plastic age came into being. The travelling tinsmiths lost their trade. In fact everything traditional was dying out, and dying out quickly. The travelling tradesmen were losing their trades in cart-making, ironwork, even horse-trading; the car, van and lorry were taking over.

'The travellers were now becoming a burden; they were not wanted at people's doors anymore. They were being reduced to beggary, but even with this they were getting it very hard to live. Thus the travelling people turned to working, to earn a few shillings. The farmers of Ireland welcomed them near their houses when they needed them for harvesting, beet pulling and potato picking.

'My father and mother, brothers and sisters worked and slaved from dawn to dusk for a few shillings a day. Oh yes, the travellers were sorely used as workers. They could not complain when they were sick and greatly undernourished. There were a lot more people than jobs. Then machines came into being and once again the travellers were not wanted. They became objects of abuse and scorn. They were pushed and shoved from place to place like one does with a herd of animals, so that we have today the likes of you, innocent and confused.

'Yes, son, when I look back over the years I shed many a

tear. I see the great injustice that is being done to all our people on the road, all due to the so-called progress of the nation. The only progress for those on the road is misery, suffering and abuse.

'Gone for ever is the great culture that belonged to the travelling people of Ireland. Make no mistake, son, we on the road are descended not from the famine era or the Cromwellian era but from the days of the kings of Ireland and their clans.

'The written history is very warped in its composition and truth. The history that has come down through the travellers, however, is more than reliable. It is told night after night around camp-fires, but, alas, today that too has ended. Progress has seen to that.

'Another thing, son,' the doll-man continued, 'a lot, if not all, of the writing that has survived from early Irish history was written by travellers. I am no scholar. I never went to school. I did, however, learn to read myself and I have travelled the world a bit, but all the time I was as I am now, in so far as I sold wares and begged my way wherever I went.

'There are things that are unique among our people on the road that even this modern age cannot change, or at least has not done so yet. One is the making of the simple tent we sleep in or the humble wagon. These are made today as they have been made for hundreds of years, even from pre-Christian times: wattles are first of all stuck into the ground, then bent into an arch and placed into little holes on a long bit of board that runs in the middle like a spinal cord. It's very simple work indeed that has remained unchanged throughout the years. For you see, the holes that are put into the board, or 'rigging pole' as it's called, are made in pairs, making ten holes in all. They are put in the pole by simply putting a small bar or poker into a fire to redden it, and then with the hot iron the holes are bored one by one. Wattles are taken from the hazel trees because of their being able to withstand the bending needed for the tunnel-like effect when they are put into the rigging pole.

The wagon, though on wheels, is made in the same way as the tent. It is, in other words, a tent on wheels, the only difference being that the wattles become benders, and it has the added comfort of being off the ground.

'These are things that did not begin yesterday, but hundreds of years ago, and with all the modern progress, they are still as simple and as useful – even the shelter tent, that simple affair of canvas which is built around an open fire to give shelter. You know, something like the Indian tepee. These are the things that historians have overlooked, or is that they want to overlook?

'These men overlook too our great scholars of the past. They skip or gloss over the wanderlust of such people as the monks in the early Christian days; St Patrick himself was a great pavvy. Then there were the Irish minstrels who travelled the country to entertain. All these men, your ancestors and mine, that is....'

'You mean,' I interrupted, 'that St Patrick and all were our relations? But why don't we have great men like these on the road now then?'

'Hold your horses, son, you're going too fast for me now,' replied the old man as he continued. 'Well I suppose one word will answer that – progress. You see, ours is a culture which has always, for mysterious reasons, been associated with the early Christian period in Ireland. This culture flourished right through the ages.

'Through its influences others learned and then, with the influx of foreigners, they broke away. They became class-conscious and aloof through greed, ambition and pride, which brought about war after war and brother fighting brother. Through all this, groups of pavvies still travelled the roads, caring nothing for castles or forts. They still plied their humble trades, travelling with the monks and priests, knowing full well that wherever these men preached, a crowd would gather, and in a crowd the travellers always sold more and begged more.

'This continues even to this day. If you go to shrines in Ireland on special days of the year, when there is a feast or pattern on, you will see travellers galore.

'I never went to school; if I had gone, even for a couple of years, I too could have written a book and probably would have become famous, but again, maybe years hence, some highly educated men would discredit it by saying someone else wrote it. This, son, is the life you are up against. This is the thing that causes the great unrest that is in the world today.

'This brings me back to you, son, because you are part of this society. I don't know what lies in store for you in future years, but I only hope that goodness comes your way. Your idea about school is a good one, but with the way us people of the road are abused and shunned it can be dangerous. I am an old man and during the past ten years or so I have seen boys like you on the road grow to manhood very disturbed indeed. A quarter of their number ended up in prisons. They have nothing but hatred and disillusionment in their hearts. Drink is their undoing and the only outlet for their shattered illusions.

'Yes son, this is what the twentieth century has brought to Ireland. For all the education and all the so-called prosperity, simplicity, love and human understanding have walked out the door. In its place we have torment, misery and degradation. It would be a great thing if we could knock back the clock four or five hundred years and be in the company of the simple and revered monks and people that were good, instead of the evil pit that is the modern era.

'I'm old, son, as is my wife, bless her. I have raised four sons, but it would have been a greater blessing if they had not been born, for they are in and out of trouble all the time. One of them is at this very moment in a mental hospital, a nervous wreck. As I look at you, I think of my lads when they were teenagers – talkative, inquisitive and innocent. Now I have nought but the wife and the dancing doll. The dancing doll I can manipulate to do my will, but with my children I was powerless. Society manipulated their lives to destruction.

'That's why I find it hard to give you advice, son. If I say you are better off on the road and you are not, I feel guilty;

the same can be said if I advise you to go to school. Either of these two ways can spell trouble, but only in this present time. You see son, life is becoming more difficult and the road as a way of life is finished. Education can be good, but under the influence of present-day standards it is useless. This is especially so for children of the road. They, unlike the settled community, have a far harder battle for survival.

'In all, son, I think the most important thing is that you gain, first of all, an understanding of your fellow man. Having this, love will truly follow. You will overcome the petty hatreds so common in our age. This, however, son, is the hardest thing of all to learn. I'm an old man, now, waiting for my Maker to call me. The one thing I regret is that I was not able to help my children, and I feel anger for the evil that is in modern society for their ruination. However, I pray – and I hope, too, in vain – that they will be able to pick up their lives again. I pray, likewise, that you too will pick up your life and that you won't be tainted by the evil around you.'

'I like the way you talk, sir,' I said to the old man. 'I like people a lot, and I pray that they will like me and all people on the road. But I would like it best of all if people kept on talking like you. That is why I used to like the chats that went on around the camp-fires on the road when everyone was sober. The same applies to the lovely sermons the priests give at Mass and at retreats. I often say to myself that I wish this could go on forever. I always feel good at times like this. But why doesn't this last? Why do people have to drink and fight and be cruel? This is what makes me want to be on my own, to be away from it all. I find it very hard, though, because I still feel lonely and miss my parents, even though, I know that I am unhappy with them. I don't know what is doing it, but I feel that I must get to school somehow. All the time I feel like this.'

'This, son,' said the doll-man, 'is all part of growing up, although I am a bit puzzled by some of your ways of thinking. I hope that your destiny will somehow be advantageous to you, and to others as well. Who knows, but

God may have chosen you especially. This is the part that a man never knows. But you must realise that being born to the road is no disgrace, for behind you is a unique culture, language and way of life that has survived for many many centuries; alas, like everything that is good in life, it's marked for doom. So what little you remember of your road days, cherish, for they will one day become golden memories. Remember this most of all, son, that not very long ago, people were happy on the road. There was a time when they were not despised or mocked, a time when there was no fighting and drunkenness. Those were the times when they were useful to the so-called civilised settled people. When their usefulness was no longer needed, they were no longer needed.'

'You know,' I said, 'I keep thinking about people. I keep asking myself, why do people have to hate each other? I keep thinking how nice it would be and how happy everyone would be if they did not hate each other. I don't know why I keep thinking like this; perhaps my father is right when he says that I'm a funny one. There are times when I go and beg from house to house for old books. I can't read, but I collect loads of these things and look through their pages for hours, wishing that I could read their contents.

'Sometimes I might get someone to read one for me, but this was not often. This only made me more anxious to be able to read myself. I also get the feeling that I would have liked to have lived in the days of the early Christian monks in Ireland. I always enjoy hearing stories about those people who lived during the Dark Ages. When I do think about these things I always feel happy and it makes me forget everything else. Is this good or does it cause me to be strange, like my father says?'

'You just go on thinking like this,' said the old man. 'It's good for you, for it helps you develop your mind and does no harm whatsoever. All I can say is that if everyone was to think in this way the world would be a far happier place to live in. Right now, son, it is late, and much as I'd like to continue chatting I can't. My aged bones get very weary these days. Tomorrow night, if you wish to stay, we will have another good chat. How about that?'

'All right,' I answered. 'I wish it was always like this. I really feel happy now sitting here, listening to you. I wish everyone in the whole world was like you, honest I do.'

'Yes, I well believe you, son, I well believe you,' said the old man, 'but as I said, tomorrow we can both be happy again with our chat.'

I was indeed happy and slept the most contented sleep that night. I loved every word the old man spoke and listened to every word as if I were in a trance. I had heard many, many people tell stories in my life but none made me feel as happy as did the doll-man that time in Kilkenny. The following night I got chatting to him again. During the day I went with the old man to the town, and whilst he made his doll dance to barrel-organ music, I collected the money for him. We had a good day's takings, and the old man was in right form for talking. His wife, however, was a very quiet old lady who rarely spoke unless spoken to. I liked her, for in a way she reminded me of my own granny.

'Well,' began the old man, 'we didn't do bad today, son, you brought me luck. I would say that was the best day I had for a long time, thanks to you.'

'It seems a funny way to hawk a town though, I mean with the doll,' I said, 'I never saw one of those before, especially with funny music.'

'No, I suppose you're right there,' said the old man. 'I suppose I am the only one doing this now. But remember the barrel organ is – and was – a well-known way of making a living. Most people who do it, though, have a monkey with them to attract the attentions of the crowds. I must be the only one, probably in the world, who uses the dancing doll. I have been at this all my life, as was my father before me, and his father before him. It's a very old thing – I mean the barrel organ and the dolls. I believe it goes back four or five hundred years.'

'I'd love to be able to do something good for people on

the road,' I said. 'You know, when I have a chat with myself now and again, I always say how I will one day be able to help my parents and other people.'

'Do you often have chats with yourself, then?' asked the old man.

'Well, yes, I do, but that is not wrong, is it?' I asked.

'Of course not,' said the old man. 'I do it myself, but I call it thinking aloud. You know you remind me about a story my grandfather told me; it was about a lad by the name of Oliver Goldsmith. Would you like to hear it?'

'Yes,' I said, 'I'd love to.'

'Well,' said the old man, 'when my grandfather's father was a mere lad – they were travelling in Meath at the time – one day a fellow riding a big dray-horse pulled up at the camp and asked if he could have something to eat as he had come a long journey and was very hungry. One of the men at the camp thought it funny that someone with a fine horse like he had should be hungry. Anyway, Oliver Goldsmith told them that he had run away from home because of some disgrace he brought on his parents.

'Of course my great-grandfather's parents felt sorry for him and made him feel quite at home. After a hearty meal he said that he would stay with them on the road for a while so that his horse could get into good condition for the remainder of the road to Cork; for it was there he said he was going, to get a boat to England to make his fortune. Well, he travelled with my great-grandfather's family for about three weeks or so, during which time he was very happy. My grandfather told me, however, that he had one habit that made the travellers he met very happy – he was a great storyteller. Besides this, he had a lovely speaking voice which always enchanted his listeners. The funny thing about the way that Oliver told stories was that he told them like poems.

'He used to – of all things – write his story first and then tell it; in all he was very well liked by the travellers, and during the three weeks he spent with my great-grandparents' family, he kept writing lots of things. Then, when they got near Cork, he decided to leave. Before he left, however, he sold his horse to my great-grandfather's parents for a few pounds. He said that with the money he would get the boat to England. He said he stole the horse from his parents but that would not stop him from obtaining the few quid he needed.

'Well, the scallywag sold the horse, and with the money and some books and his writing he left for England. And,' continued the old man, 'he wasn't many years in England when he became famous as a poet and writer; when he returned to Ireland he tried to trace the travellers who were so good to him, but without success.'

'Thus the man became not Oliver Goldsmith the rascal, but Oliver Goldsmith, poet. He wrote many great works and undoubtedly his finest was the 'Vicar of Wakefield', but, as you can see, he could've stayed on the road. Either way he would have become great.

'He was greatly admired by the travellers for his devil-may-care ways, even as the learned man that he was. So that is why I'd say that you could be like him one day. You are such a dreamer and so full of ideas that I have never seen a lad like you before. I feel sure that with a bit of education you could become great and famous. You know, son, I would like if a lad like you or someone else off the road, could one day become famous. It would be good to get back to the beauty of learning like in the days of long ago. It was then, my lad, that the people of the road were an example and a heritage to be proud of. Today, alas, we are treated and looked upon as ignorant savages.'

'You like the travellers a lot, don't you?' I asked the old man. 'I do too, and that is why I'd like to get myself educated. So after this I mean to go to school, somehow. I'll keep going to church and to the missions, because they are great for the talks and sermons they give. If only I could read though; I keep trying but I can't make the letters out and this makes me almost cry. If only you or some other traveller could read, it wouldn't be too bad because I could learn from them or you.'

'Indeed, son, if I could read well I'd only too willingly

teach you. But most of what I know comes from listening to tales around the camp-fire. People say that I sound and talk like an educated man, and when I tell them I can read and write only a little they can't believe it. So you see I do hope that you, one day, will be granted this blessing by the grace of God.'

'Will you die by the roadside?' I asked suddenly.

'Will I die by the roadside? What are you talking about?' asked the doll-man. 'What on earth makes you ask such a question? If you really want to know, I hope so, but really I don't know where I shall die.'

'Oh, I didn't mean anything wrong,' I explained, 'it's just that I wouldn't like to see you waked by the roadside.'

'Waked by the roadside?' asked the old man, very puzzled. 'What on earth are you talking about? You really are a strange one, I can see that now.'

'I was merely thinking of a wake that took place some time ago on the road. I didn't like it and I hope I never see one again. It was a woman who died and she was laid out in the tent she died in. There were two candles lit, one on either side of her head. It was terrible looking at her white face, which was very frightening in the pale candle-light. There were several travelling families sitting around the fireside outside the tent that night. They started the night by telling haunted stories, which made the whole thing even worse.

'After this they began talking about the dead woman, telling how good she was. Then one or two of the womenfolk started to cry, and suddenly all around the fire began not crying, but keening, sounding just like a greyhound baying. This continued for hours without a stop, in fact until the break of day. This went on for three nights. I did not stay at the fire after the first night; I went to my own tent to sleep, but I could not. As I lay there the white face, lit up by the candles, kept appearing before my eyes. I kept thinking about the dead woman and how lonely she looked. It did not seem right to keep that poor woman's body lying there in the tent for three nights and days. I was happy when it was all over. So you see, I would never like to see anything like that again. That is why I would not like to think of you dying by the roadside.'

'Son,' said the old man, 'seeing such things is nothing to worry about. This is all part of life. We all must die and when we do there are always people who miss us very much. A wake is to show this. It is meant as a mark of respect for people we love who have gone to meet their Maker. You, of course, are shocked by what you saw because it was possibly the first time you saw such a wake. As you grow older you will not notice this, it will not shock you but become part of living, part of everyday life.

'Speaking of wakes, son,' said the doll-man, 'reminds me of me own father, Lord rest him. Now he died on the roadside and was waked and buried on a little back road outside the village of Oranmore. This custom has died out now, son. It is a pity that the poor travellers can't be buried like they used to be years ago.'

'I heard about this,' I interrupted, 'but I could not believe it, I mean, being buried at the roadside. It doesn't seem right.'

'Why of course it's right, son,' said the old man. 'There's nothing more fitting for the travellers than to be buried on the roadside where they have been born and lived throughout their lives, the road they love so much. Thanks be to God, Ireland's roads hold many marks as the last resting places of many weary travellers who passed away to meet their Maker, God rest them all.

'I always think it wrong to be buried in the large drab graveyards that are part of this age. They are desolate indeed for a person on the road. So I too would like to be buried at some good camping-ground by the roadside. I would rest happy, then, knowing that other travellers would make their camp near where I lay. As things are now, I shall more than likely end up in a pauper's grave, alone and forgotten; but there, son, is life; death is another thing.'

'You know, sir,' I said, 'tomorrow I am going to head back towards home. I miss my family a lot, but I will try first if I can get some chance to go to school.'

'Well, son,' said the old man, 'I think you should stay with me and the wife for a while. It is, of course, your choice. But, whatever you decide to do, remember to cherish life as a blessing from God; if you do this, then life will treat you with respect.'

That night I spent a restless night thinking on the advice of the old man and what I was going to do now. I thought a lot about how my family was and what their plight might be. I knew, though, that going home would not be good. I knew that my running away would have been in vain. No, my decision was to continue my wanderings, wanderings that were, however, to be but for a short time. Most of all they were *not* to be in vain.

8

I left the doll-man and his wife to start out on my lone journey. I did not, however, head towards home, but for some mysterious reason, started out in the opposite direction, eventually ending up in County Waterford. I headed for Cappoquin and the monastery of Mount Melleray. I had been here many years before with my mother and now I wanted to visit it again. I was fascinated when I heard about the monks here and how they never spoke. I heard too that they had to dig a bit of their own graves each day.

When I got to the monastery the monks gave me a meal. After this I went to chapel; here I watched the monks at prayer. As they chanted I could feel goose-pimples all over my body. I loved listening to their voices as they stood in lines, their cowls pulled over their heads. The organ music was heavenly to hear. I was so overcome by the scene I began whispering to myself.

'Oh, I wish I could feel as happy as this always. This is like heaven. Oh, Lord,' I cried, 'why can't I be like these monks?'

The monks around me continued their prayers, undisturbed by my presence. After praying for some time, tears began to well up in my eyes. With a heavy heart I left the church and the monastery and started on the lonely walk back to Waterford. Even on the road again the tears still welled up in my eyes.

'Oh, my God, why do I have to feel so alone? What can I do to help myself and my family? I seem to be doomed to failure. I should never have left my home. But I can't go back now.'

I was breaking my young heart trying to find a way to overcome the great loneliness and feeling of isolation. Little did I know that within a matter of weeks my prayers were to be answered, and in a way that I had never even given a thought to.

I had reached Waterford and from there made my way to the seaside resort of Tramore. It was late August and Tramore was crowded with holiday-makers. I stayed there about a week, hanging around. Then I got ill from sleeping on the beach. All my clothes were in ribbons. I had not eaten for many a day. I was in a poor state when I was found asleep on the beach of Tramore by a garda one night. I was taken to a garda station and a doctor was called. As a result I was immediately transferred to hospital, very undernourished and suffering from pneumonia.

For many weeks I remained in the hospital, so ill that I never realised where I was. Gradually I recovered, but for many days after did not speak a word. I had, of course, become aware of my surroundings, but still would not speak. Then one morning the doctor who had been attending me throughout the illness spoke to me in his usual manner to try to get me to talk.

'Hey, little fellow,' he asked 'how are you doing today? Still silent, are you? I will say, though, that you look really well today. Can you hear me talk, son? If you can hear me, nod your head.'

'Yes,' I said, 'I can hear you.'

'Well, I never,' said the doctor, 'I just can't believe it. You know that those are the first words I have ever heard you speak and you have been here for more than six weeks now.'

'Are my parents here?' I asked. 'Am I going back to them again?'

'Your parents?' said the doctor, taken aback. 'But we don't even know your name, lad, let alone where your parents are.'

'Oh, my name's Sean Devine and I left my parents a long time ago – you see I want to go to school.'

'Oh you do, do you?' said the doctor, still more puzzled, 'And where, may I ask you, have you been since you left your parents?'

'I've been travelling around on my own,' I said.

'Do you know where you are now?' asked the doctor.

'No,' I said, 'where am I?'

'Well,' said the doctor, 'you are in hospital, because over the past weeks you have been very, very sick, but you are well now, thank God. We could not get in touch with your parents because we were unable to find out who you are or where you came from.'

'I would rather go to school than go home. You won't send me home, will you?' I pleaded.

'Listen, son, you would be better off at home than going around the road on your own. You must remember that you almost died, and this mustn't happen to a nice young lad like you, must it?'

'What's going to happen now? Are you going to send me back to my parents or not?' I asked.

'Now listen, lad,' said the doctor, 'you have no need to worry; if it's school you want, then school you'll get, but for now you must get really well. Now you must promise that you will get well first.'

'Okay,' I said, 'I promise, but I do want to go to school.'

I stayed another two weeks at the hospital, and during this time my parents were located and informed about my being found and about my illness. They wanted to come and see me, but were told that it would be in my best interest if I went to school for some years. They were told that this was my reason for having run away. They were told that if they took me back now I would run away again and would end up as I was now.

My father wanted me back, but my mother wanted to take the doctor's advice. Thus, after much discussion by telephone – for my parents were over eighty miles away at the time – it was agreed that I could go to school until the age of sixteen.

I did not know of the battle that had been going on on my behalf, but was told that I would be going to school. The doctor talked to me about it one morning.

'Well, me wandering hermit,' he said to me, 'you are

going to school, you won't need to wander any more. Are you glad?'

'Oh yes, I'm glad; but what about my parents?' I asked.

'Oh, that's all right,' said the doctor, 'they know all about it and they are glad too.'

'Even my father?' I asked.

'Even your father,' affirmed the doctor.

'You know, sir, God didn't forget, did he?' I asked. 'I feel very happy now. I wonder will it take me long to learn to read and write. Now I shall be a priest, you wait and see. Then I can help my family – in fact, I'll help every poor person. When will I go to school?'

'You'll go within the next few days,' said the doctor.

I was about to start school and fulfil my childish ambition. However, I never did realise the great agony and torment and sleepless nights I had caused my parents whilst I was roaming the roads, particularly my mother. She hoped against hope that she would get word of my whereabouts. Every traveller she met she would ask if they had seen her son. My father started drinking again, to try to forget about my mysterious disappearance. When they got the news of my being found, it seemed like a miracle. Though they were many miles away they were still happy that I had been found alive. They agreed to everything that had been asked of them as regards my being sent to school. Though they would miss me for the years I would be away, they were so overcome with excitement that they forgot it.

I eventually reached St Joseph's Industrial School in Cork city; I was, for an instant, disappointed. At first sight it was a large, dismal-looking, red-brick building. Even when I entered its polished hallway I wasn't impressed; on meeting the Superior, however, I was. Behind a polished desk sat a very kind-looking grey-haired man, who spoke in a gentle voice.

'So you are the young gentleman who longs to be at school?' he said to me.

'Yes, sir,' I said timidly.

'Good,' said the Superior, 'but I would like you to call

me "Brother", as do all the boys here. First of all, young man, I suppose it's only proper that I know your name, then we will be the wiser for our manners.'

'My name is Sean Devine, s..., I mean Brother,' I said.

'Sean Devine,' said the Superior. 'Well Sean, you should like our school and I hope very much that you will be happy here. What is your age by the way? I've got all the other details here, but not your age.'

'I'm nine,' I lied.

'Oh, you are big for your age,' said the Superior. 'I suppose you don't know the date of your birth?'

'No, Brother,' I said, 'I only know that I was nine last January.'

'Oh well, never mind, this will not be difficult to find out. Now let Michael Alken here show you to the dining-room. In fact, Michael, you can show Sean all around the school and be his guide and helper until he gets used to us. Do you understand, Michael?'

'Yes, Brother,' said the boy who had walked into the study.

'Very well then; now, Sean, meet Michael who will be your guide and help you to get used to our school routine. He will verse you well, so don't be frightened to ask him questions, or me for that matter. We are here to help you, always remember this; you can both go now.'

'Thank you, Brother,' I said, and left the study with my guide, Michael Alken; 'Know-all', as I was to learn later, was his nickname.

I had taken an instant liking to Michael, who was nine years old. He looked very studious for his age. He brought me to the dining-room and to the table where he sat.

'This will be your table, Sean, for all your meals; you can sit next to me, because I am a monitor. In fact, I shall be your monitor whilst you remain at this table,' said Michael.

'Monitor? What's that?' I asked.

'Oh, that means a person in charge. You see,' Michael explained, 'every table has a monitor; as you can see, there are eight boys to each table and one boy is appointed as monitor by the Superior.'

'Oh,' I said, 'I see.'

'Anyway,' said Michael, 'you'll soon get the hang of it.'

Besides Michael, there were six other boys at my table, who all had nicknames; they were: Barracha, Tags, Busang, Tomato Jack, Lame Duck and Bucka. They were all around the same age as Michael, between nine and ten. I was very struck by the nicknames, and even years afterwards I did not know some of the boys by their real names. In fact, nearly everyone in the school had a nickname, including the teachers. I was soon to learn all of them, and a lot more besides.

For the first week or so I did not go to class at all but spent my time going around the whole building with Michael, meeting all the Brothers and getting to know the whole place.

I got on with and liked Michael very well; in fact, within days we became the best of friends and were to remain so for the duration of the time I was at St Joseph's. As we got to know each other I asked Michael loads and loads of questions.

'Where do you come from, Michael?'

'From Waterford. I have been here three years now. I go home for six weeks, holidays each summer. You'll be able to go home too.'

'I don't think so,' I said. 'You see, my parents don't live in a house, they are travellers.'

'Oh,' said Michael in surprise.

9

I will always remember Michael Alken's 'Oh' of surprise when he first learned that my parents were travellers. It has typified for me Irish people's attitude towards us pavvies. We are different, not by creed or colour but by an indefinable something with which settled people have not come to terms. Michael knew that his reply had hurt and he tried to make amends

'I didn't know that, but allow me to tell you not to say it to any of the other boys here because if you do, they will kick you and you won't like it. I don't mind myself, but you'll do well to take my advice. Say you live anywhere, but not on the road.'

Thus I had to get used to being a boy from a respectable way of life rather than the more humble abode by the roadside. It sounded simple at first, but as the weeks went by I found it a strain until, with the help of my new-found friend, I soon got used to, and even mastered the difficulty.

Another acute embarrassment that I had to overcome was the start to my education, and this proved the most difficult of all. I could not read or write one single word when I arrived at St Joseph's. So, to begin my schooling, I had to start in the infants' class. This, of course, meant being called 'baby' by the other boys in the school. Outwardly I did not seem to mind, but inwardly I felt the hurt of it. Luckily enough, I had a good ally in the form of Brother Columba, or 'Left Law', as he was known by the boys.

Brother Columba taught infants and first standard in the one large classroom, and when he got a big lad like me – I was really twelve years old – he was presented with a problem. Unwittingly, however, in the end I was to become my own succour, though I did not realise it at the time. It all began at a singing lesson one day when I was asked by Brother Columba why I wasn't joining in. I told the brother quite innocently:

'I don't like the songs they sing in this school, Brother, there're not nice, especially the foolish Irish one about the boat in the sea.'

'Oh,' said Brother Columba calmly, 'and pray, minstrel, have you a better song to sing for us?'

'Of course I know better songs,' I said proudly, 'I know plenty that's better.'

'Then,' said the brother, 'perhaps you will sing some of these better songs of yours, because we would love to hear them.'

'All right, then, I'll sing the "Wild Colonial Boy" first,' I said.

> 'There was a wild Colonial boy, Jack Duggan was his
> name,
> He was born and reared in Ireland, in a place called
> Castlemaine,
> He was his father's only pride, his mother's pride and
> joy
> And dearly did his parents love the Wild Colonial Boy.'

After singing this song, everyone clapped and I was asked to sing another.

> 'I don't give a damn, for gaiging is the best,
> For when a feen is corrped, sure he has a little rest.
> Sure he's got a little molly and he's got a little beor,
> And it's off on the tober, with his molly and his beor.
>
> By night around the glimmer, when the gallias are 'n
> lee,
> You can see him dance a merry step a' there for you 'n
> me.
> He doesn't have to worry and he doesn't have to care,
> So long as he's got a sark for his old grey mare.'

This song had them all puzzled, because the words of it were quite strange. When I was asked if I knew the meaning of the words, I said I didn't. I knew that if I did so I would have to explain a lot of things besides the words of the song. The song, in ordinary words, goes as follows:

'I don't give a damn, for beggin is the best
For when a man is tired, sure he has a little rest.
Sure he's got a little tent and he's got a little woman,
And it's off on the road, with his tent and his woman.

By night around the fire, when the children are in
    bed,
You can see him dance a merry step for either you or
    me,
He doesn't have to worry and he doesn't have to care,
So long as he's a field for his old grey mare.'

These songs went down well with everyone in the classroom, and when I told the stories about the ghosts, on another occasion, I was even more popular. I told the story of the cats in the graveyard and others I had heard on the road.

I became part of the school in no time. I was accepted by the other boys there, without the usual reception that is set aside for boys who enter St Joseph's for the first time. I had of course to learn to adjust myself to a way and routine of life that was completely alien to me. I was gravely handicapped by my lack of any type of previous schooling, but, as if by a miracle, by the time I was six months at the school, I was able to read and write fluently.

The method of teaching practised at the school was in my opinion, silly, and I said this too, to Brother Columba. In first standard they had a very simple beginners' book and it was this that I objected to. Usually Brother Columba would sit in the front of the class and read a phrase from the book; then he would get all the class to look at their books and repeat it together aloud. He would do this many times and then ask each boy, in turn, to repeat the phrase. When it came to my turn, I stood up as the others had done and read from my book, aloud:

'It is so wet a day, that I cannot go out to play..., and I don't care anyhow whether it's wet or dry, I'm tired listening to it,' I said.

'Devine,' said Brother Columba, 'the first thirteen words you read were correct but the rest don't happen to be in the book.'

'I know, Brother,' I said, 'but I get tired listening about the wet day and play. I would like if it was a story instead.'

'Devine, you will now step up here to the front of the class,' said the Brother.

I did so, and was given three slaps for my insolence. I returned to my seat to continue my lessons. The following week, however, I was put in another class where I was given a new school reader. The teacher in second class was Brother Theobald.

When he started reading the book to the class I fell in love with it straight away. In it were stories of Setanta, Fionn Mac Cumhaill, Cuchulainn, the Children of Lir and others. Here at last was my world, and the moment I heard them I was learning, and did not look back.

Within a short time I was moved up another standard, to third class, under the guidance of Brother Eugene. There is no doubt that it was the book of stories that created my interest in learning. Somehow the tales of Setanta, Tír-na-nÓg and the like seemed very familiar to me. Somewhere I had heard these tales before, when I was on the road. Only the characters were different.

Brother Eugene was a man of fifty who had spent thirty or so of those years in the order of the Presentation Brothers. He was different from the other brothers in that he spoke with an English accent. He never taught Irish or singing, which made me quite happy. He was a man who loved English literature, and was forever telling stories and reading. Brother Eugene first became interested in me one day when he recited a poem by Longfellow to the class.

'Today,' Brother Eugene said, 'we are going to recite "The Village Blacksmith" by Henry Wadsworth Longfellow; I want to know whether you like it or not, and most important, why you like or dislike it.

After reciting the first verse of the poem, Brother Eugene asked if any boy in the class had heard the poem before.

'Yes, Brother,' I said, 'I could say that first verse easy.'

'Why, did you learn it before, then?' asked the Brother.

'No, Brother, but I like it, 'cause I used to know lots of blacksmiths.'

'Well, in that case, let's hear you reciting the first verse,' said the brother.

'Under a spreading chestnut tree the village smithy
    stands,
The smith, a mighty man is he, with large and sinewy
    hands,
The muscles of his brawny arms are as strong as iron
    bands,
His hair is crisp, black and long and his face is like the
    tan,
And he looks the whole world in the face for he owes
    not any man.'

'Are you sure,' asked the brother, 'that you never learned this before?'

'Yes, Brother, I am sure that was the first time I ever heard it, but I do like it,' I answered.

When I sat down, the whole class was as silent as night, and all eyes were glued on me.

'Now, suppose I were to read out the whole poem to you, do you think you would be able to do the same, reciting it all?'

'I don't know,' I said. 'I expect I could. At least I could try.'

Brother Eugene read out the three verses from the book. When he had finished, I walked up to the front of the class and recited the whole poem word for word. Brother

Eugene was amazed at my performance and was not slow in letting the whole class know it.

'This is very good for you, Sean,' he said. Then to the class he said, 'Isn't he very good, boys?' The whole class answered 'Yes' in unison.

From that day on, Brother Eugene was to take an exceptional interest in me and develop my gift for learning. I loved every moment of the lessons I received from him for, whilst most of the boys in my class were still learning their ABC, I was delving into the classics under his guidance. In point of fact, Brother Eugene began teaching me after school, in the library. It was at such times that I could pour out questions without hindrance from my fellow classmates. Here too, in private, I was able to talk to him about road life and about my hatred of it.

At one of these sessions Brother Eugene said to me, 'Sean, you are a very remarkable boy. You have an unquenchable thirst for learning. Can you tell me why?'

'Oh, because I like it,' said I, 'particularly your stories, although some of the stories you tell are different from the ones I heard at home.'

'And how do you mean "different", Sean?' asked Brother Eugene.

'Ah, like St Patrick and that. You never tell about him being a traveller, like I was told on the road.'

'That is because you may have heard a false version,' said Brother Eugene.

'No, it was not false, it's the one in the schoolbook that's wrong, because St Patrick was a travelling man,' I replied.

'With Irish history, English, Danish and what have you, perhaps yours is not false, after all. There is one thing I want you to do, Sean, and that is to tell me some more of your stories about the past, the ones you have heard around the camp-fires I mean. Will you do that?'

'Yes, Brother,' I said, 'I will tell you lots if you want me to.'

Thus I continued my questions. After the first year at school I had mastered reading, and in so doing read very widely about Ireland and its religious and literary history.

'Brother,' I said to my favourite teacher one day, 'in all the history books I have read of Ireland and England, there is never a word mentioned about the travellers.'

'Maybe,' said the Brother politely, 'there were no travellers then.'

'Oh but there were,' I said. 'Even St Patrick used to travel with them, as well as the monks and the priests.'

'Yes, Sean, this may have been so, but the history of any country is very hard to pin-point, especially that of many centuries ago. You must always remember that there were not many educated men in those days and you have to be very well educated to write any history.'

'This isn't true,' I said, 'nearly every famous writer or poet of the past had hardly any education.'

'And who, may I ask you, told you that?' asked the Brother.

'Oh, a very old friend of mine on the road; he was old, too, so he should know,' I answered.

'Well to a certain extent, I suppose I shall have to grant you that.'

Three or four times a year, at such times as Easter, Christmas and Hallowe'en, I received a parcel from my mother. Whenever I got a parcel it always made me a bit depressed. For it made me think and worry about my parents, especially my mother. I kept thinking of all the walking and begging she had to do in order to be able to send the parcel.

With my pal Michael, who had a very great influence on me, I would discuss the future and what it would have in store for both of us. Michael was a very intelligent lad for his years; like me, he was forever reading books. We found out a great deal about each other because we talked freely about our past.

'You know, Michael,' I said, on one of our walks together, 'I would love to know what I could do when I grow up. I keep thinking that I may have to go back to travelling with my parents, but I only hope to God I don't.'

'Oh, you won't have to do that,' said Michael, 'you can

please yourself when you leave here. I know that I won't go home when I do. Instead, I shall get a job and earn lots of money.'

'That would be no good to me,' I said, 'because the money would be spent in no time. I'd like to become a priest or a teacher, then I could travel all over the world. My parents would like this because they'd know that I could help them then.'

'Sean,' asked Michael suddenly, 'what is it like living on the road?'

'At times,' I answered, 'it's hell; other times it can be heaven, but unfortunately it's more often hell than heaven.'

'Why is it that the travellers seem to fight all the time?' asked Michael.

'I suppose it's the drink really,' I said. 'People get very cross and wicked when they get drunk and that's why they fight. Mammy said that drink's a curse and makes people bad. I'll never drink when I grow up because of this.'

'Yeah,' said Michael, 'I think you're right there, but if it's a curse, why do people drink it?'

'I don't know,' said I, 'I suppose it's because when they taste it they can't help it.'

'What about the heavenly times, though?' asked Michael.

'Yes, the heavenly times,' I murmured. 'Well, to tell you the truth, these were very few. These were the times when it was early spring and mid-summer. At times like this it's nice living on the road. It's also nice when you are sitting by a large camp-fire listening to stories being told.'

'What kind of stories?' asked Michael.

'Oh, every kind of story, and all of them true,' I said.

'Could you tell us one of these stories?' asked Michael eagerly.

'I could tell you hundreds. Indeed, there are so many I don't know which one to begin with. I know, I'll tell you the one about the Blessed Well near Cahir in County Tipperary. I know this one is true, because I was there the night it happened.

'It all began,' I said, 'in the old camping road about half

129

a mile from the town of Cahir. I was only eight or nine years old at the time, but I remember it as if it were yesterday. Now, near this old camping road there was a fast-flowing river, and it used to be a favourite place for us to swim in. Well, we pulled into this old road to camp for a few days. Some other travellers had arrived just ahead of us. Anyway, my father picked up a firm bit of ground and built the tent.

'That night we had a roaring fire of sticks and a good few of the other travelling men and women came down to sit around our fire for a chat.

'Anyway, what with all the pots of tea and the continuous chat, the small hours of the morning had crept in unnoticed. Then, God save us, things began to happen. My father picked up the kettle-bar to sink into the ground over the fire to boil the kettle for some more tea.

'He lifted the bar into the air to give him some force to sink the pointed end of it into the ground. As the bar hit the ground, everyone heard a very loud noise, the unmistakable sound of metal hitting wood. Although everyone heard the noise they all forgot it almost immediately it happened. My father said it was just a lump of buried wood, so he left the bar in the ground and hung the kettle on it to boil over the fire.

'Now comes the strange part,' I continued. 'The kettle had been on the fire for no more than a second when it started boiling mad. Everyone looked at it in amazement. "Well I'm sure I just put that kettle on the fire a second or two ago and there it is boiling mad!" said my father. "Here, let one of the children go to the river for another can of water whilst I take off this kettle."

'Well,' I continued, 'one of the children got another can of water which was then put on the fire where it too boiled immediately. Well you can imagine the surprise on everyone's face around the fire that night. "Here," said my father, "get another can of water; there must be something funny about that water."

'In due course, another can of water was brought. Then my father removed most of the fuel from the fire, leaving it barely alight. "Now," my father said, "I bet it won't boil as quick now."

'Well,' I continued, 'no sooner had the new can of cold water been put on the nearly quenched fire when it too began to boil. Now when this happened everyone gasped in amazement and, as they watched, the can began to boil over. But as it boiled over, the water was red. Yes,' I said, 'red like blood.'

'When everyone around the fire saw this they became frightened and asked my father to take the can off the fire. My father did so, and as he put the can down on the grass near the fire some of the contents spilled on his hand. My father of course pulled back his hand, afraid of the scalding water. But, strange as it may seem, he had felt no pain. Then, in front of everyone, he dipped his finger into the can and took it out again. His finger was covered in blood. "It's cold," said my father, "it's stone cold".

' "What in the name of God is it?" asked one of the men at the fire. "God save us, it's a sign."

'My father then began moving the kettle bar. "Right," he said, "get that fire lit up again and get a couple of old spades; I want to see what's in the ground under that bar."

'Well,' I continued, 'the fire was soon blazing again and beneath its bright light, my father and a few other men began digging the ground where the bar had been sunk. After about twenty minutes' digging they uncovered what appeared to be a large, long box with a lid on it. After further digging the whole box was laid bare. Then, very quickly my father lifted its lid and everyone who stood around gasped and moaned in sheer fright.

'My father almost fainted at the sight before his eyes. Even I turned away; in fact, I was told later that I screamed when the box was opened.

'Well, even now when I think of it, I can fully realise that I had very good reason to scream that night. For there, lying in that forlorn and ordinary box, was the body of a woman with a baby in her arms. She was dead – there was no mistake about this. The lines on her face told us she was a travelling woman. To look at her and the baby you would have thought that she had only died yesterday.

'All the travellers that were there that night got on their knees and began praying for the repose of the soul of the poor woman and her baby. No one around the fire that night knew the dead woman, they had never seen her before.

'After saying the prayers, it was decided to re-cover the mother and child and leave them in their last resting place. Then, as if from thin air, everyone heard a mysterious voice that was soft and plaintive: "Please remove the mortal remains of my baby and myself from this watery grave, this unhallowed ground. Move us to a spot near the blessed well, which you will find if you to go the top of this lane and cross the main road to the little grove that will face you. When you enter the grove, follow a little worn footpath which will lead you to the well, which is close by an old lime-kiln. Here lay us to final rest."

'Everyone heard these words and became terribly frightened; but as if moved by automation, the box containing the two bodies was carried to the well which the voice had described. The travelling menfolk then dug a little grave and interred the bodies of the dead woman and her child, after which everyone said a few prayers for the repose of their souls. Then everyone returned to their respective camps where they discussed the strange happenings of the night until the first light of day.

'Strange as it may seem, no one ever found out who the dead people had been, other than that they were travellers.

'To this day, travellers go to this well to offer up their private prayers, and if you ever go there you will see lots of little souvenirs left by travellers over the years, such as rags, beads, medals and other little articles.'

'Did you really see this, Sean? I mean, were you really there?' asked Michael.

'Well, to tell you the truth,' I said, 'it wasn't me who was there, but my father. He told me the story. It is true though, I swear it. If you ever go there, you will see this well and near it a little wooden cross over where the woman and her baby are buried.'

'But why weren't the woman and baby buried in a proper graveyard?' asked Michael.

'Oh, I knew you'd ask that,' I said. 'The answer is quite simple. You see, for years and years, travelling people who died by the roadside were nearly always buried there after their wake. This was a custom that came down through the ages.'

'But this doesn't seem right,' said Michael. 'It seems completely wrong to me, being buried by the roadside, without a cross or tombstone.'

'Ah that's where you are wrong,' I said. 'They do have crosses and even tombstones erected to their memory. And that reminds me of another interesting story about the real beginnings of crosses being erected over graves.

'I don't know whether or not you know about the little crosses you can see erected on the side of the highways and by-ways of Ireland. Have you seen one?' I asked.

'Oh yes,' said Michael, 'I've seen many of these, but they are not meant as marks of graves by the roadside. You see, they are put there to mark the spot where someone was killed or died.'

'Yes,' I said, 'this happens now. But it was the travellers who first started this custom. Whenever they buried anyone by the roadside they always marked it with a little cross of some description. In the very early times they used to make mounds of earth which would be added to by other travellers who passed the place. Then, when the monks and religious came, they put large stone slabs on the spot, eventually turning to the symbol of Christianity, the cross.'

School, for me, was a godsend. I enjoyed every day I spent there, mostly for the learning. Reading books was my earthly heaven. 'All's well that ends well'; alas, with me this was not to be. Soon, like a cork, I was to be tossed out on the ocean of life. I was to be pared, as is the wattle, to support the rigging pole, and to become, in other words, a cog in the wheel.

I could not voice against this for to do so was like the clucking hen voicing the linnet. To the tober I was born, and to the tober I must return.

10

It was on a bright March day in 1948 that I left St Joseph's, to return once more to the road. A week or two before I left, my father came to collect me. However, because of the uncertainty regarding my age, he had to return home to get my birth certificate. According to the school records I was only thirteen years old, while my father, who was right, claimed I was sixteen.

When I arrived at the station at Dara after my long journey from Cork, I was greeted by a much older mother, a mother with a haggard face. Her lonely eyes were misted with tears, as were mine.

'Oh, son,' she said, 'you have changed, but it's lovely to see you.'

'You have changed too, Mammy,' I said, 'but why the tears?'

'Oh, alannah, I'm happy, that's all,' she said.

My family had grown since I last saw them. I was meeting a new brother and sister for the first time. On the first night home I had a very busy time telling all the family about my school years. I had to tell them everything that happened from the time, long ago, when I first left home until I left the school.

'Well, Bridie, alannah,' said my father, 'we have a scholar in the family now, but being a scholar isn't much good for the tober.'

'Ah whisht, you and your mooching. I'm fed up with you and your mooching. A fat lot of it you do. In all the time I'm with you, you hardly ever gave me a penny to put a bit of grub in the children's mouth, you lazy article you. No, you have no room to talk about scholars or mooching, Mickeen.'

'Faith and I'll do less too, for you or them. Your scholar son there ran when he was any good to us.'

'Yes, that's just like you, you lousy slag you. Wantin' the children to go out and beg to keep you in drink. My God, how can we have luck or grace with an article like you for a husband and father.'

'That'll do you now, mouthie, or I'll soon put me fist in your teeth,' cried my father. 'Your darling scholar son there will have to get used to mooching now; his holiday is over. And if he doesn't, I'll break his back for him.'

'You will, will you?' asked my mother. 'Well, let me tell you Mickeen, that if you lay a hand on him I'll have you taken in. You gave him enough beatings years ago, you almost drove him into an idiot. Well, not any more you won't, and I'll see to that. I'll get Sean into a trade very soon, please God, and he'll be far better off than to turn out a lazy hound like you.'

'Oh, get him what you like, and even better, why don't you and the rest of the curs go and join him?'

'I've got news for you, then, that is what I do intend to do very shortly now. I'll get Sean here to write for a house for me and the children, and to hell with you. I swear it, and nothing will change my mind, I can tell you that.'

'Good,' said my father, 'and good riddance to you and them. I can make out for myself as I did very well before I ever met you.'

'Bad luck to you, sure you hadn't even a shirt on your back when I met you, until my poor mother, God be good to her, gave you one.'

'That'll do you now, woman, and don't get my rag up; just keep that mouth of yours shut and do what you like.'

I, as well as my brothers and sisters, heard this rowing between our parents, just as it had been going on for years and years. This especially disturbed me now, because I had been but a matter of days out of school. I saw that my father still resented me. As the weeks and months went by I was always listening to such arguments between my parents. My mother tried various places in an effort to get me into some kind of trade, but without any success.

Within a year of my leaving the school I became very

unsettled, and uppermost in my mind was the problem of getting away from road life. I wanted to do something definite in life, to get some kind of decent job. I knew that whilst still living on the roadside this was impossible. Above all, I was not able to get on with my parents, and this was the thing that hurt me most.

Around the year 1950, we moved to Mullatty, in County Kildare. We had been camping for a year in an old lane near local farmers, doing casual work. During that year I wrote, on behalf of my parents, to the local county council, asking for a house. I filled out many forms and sent them away. Success came eventually; my parents got notification that they were getting a house.

The house was an old two-storey affair, with three rooms upstairs and one room and kitchen downstairs. It had a toilet and tap but no bathroom or bath. It had a large, old-type range, but no other usable fireplaces in any of the rooms.

The first thing we did when we got the key of the house was to move our wagon into the yard adjoining the house. On one side was a terrace of small houses, to which our house was attached. In front of the houses there was a large open space bordered by a river. We parked our wagon right in front of our house, where it remained for six months or more. My father said he would not part with it until he had given the house a good trial.

When we moved into the house we didn't have a stick of furniture, not even a bedstead. All we had were the three old straw mattresses we used in the wagon and some old blankets and coats we used as covering. We took these into the house, however, and tried to manage as best we could. At the time we moved into this house there were nine of us in the family; my parents, my six brothers and sisters and myself.

The first thing we did when we got into the house was to inspect every inch of the place in great excitement. It was a thing to be excited about, even for my parents. I remember very vividly what my mother said after the inspection: 'Well, it doesn't look much, but it'll do me until the end of my days, anyway. We'll soon knock it into shape when we get a few old beds and a lock of clothes for them. There's no hurry with the furniture, a few old orange boxes will do for the time being.' Then she turned to me and my brothers and said: 'The first thing ye must get is a bundle of good dry straw for your own bed upstairs. The girls can stay with me and your father downstairs until we get some proper beds.'

That same afternoon my brothers and I walked about a mile outside the town and begged two big bundles of straw. When we got home my mother had a great fire going, as well as a great feed of potatoes, meat and cabbage.

The first meal we ate, sitting on the floor of our new house, was one we all enjoyed; it was a meal under a solid roof. As my mother often said, 'there's nothing in the world equal to a meal in your belly and a roof over your head.' There was no electricity so we had to make do with the oil lamps we used in the wagon and some candles. After the meal, my mother made beds on the floor with the straw. She made one upstairs for me and my brothers, one for her and my father and one for my sisters. During the day, with the few pounds she had, she bought four or five blankets in a second-hand shop.

Bedtime came, and with it nightmares. When my brothers, Mickeeny, who was fourteen years old, Tommy, twelve, and Paudge, nine, and I blew out the candles to retire for the night, things began to happen. I was just beginning to doze off when Paudge whispered: 'Sean, are you awake? Do you hear me?' and he nudged me in the back.

'Of course I hear you,' I said. 'I'm tired hearing you day and night. What ails you, anyway? Are the fleas biting you?'

'No, Sean, I can't sleep,' muttered Paudge.

'Why can't you sleep?' I asked him.

'I'm afraid, that's why,' he said. 'This is a haunted house. I heard noises at the window and I heard footsteps too.'

'I heard them too, Sean,' said Tommy, who was also awake.

'Listen, the pair of you,' I said, 'there's no ghosts or anything else either in this house. What you probably heard was an old comeragh or creeper.'

'Well, creeper or no creeper, I'm going down to the others!' cried Tommy.

'So am I,' said Paudge. 'I don't like it up here. It's too lonely for my liking.'

Without another word the two of them dashed down the stairs and I must confess I wasn't far behind them. When all three of us landed in our parents' room, we got a good old telling off.

'You're worse, Sean,' said my mother, 'a big fellow like you, afraid of your own shadow. Go on now, the three of you, and let us get a bit of sleep.'

After all the arguing, we didn't go back upstairs, but slept, all three of us, on the kitchen floor near the door of our parents' room. In fact, we slept every night for nearly six months in the kitchen. None of us would sleep in any of the rooms upstairs. I expect the main reason for this fear of the upstairs rooms was that we had been used to being together in the wagon on the road. The strangeness and largeness of the house made it a very frightening place for all of us.

Over the first few years the house became a great trial for my parents, and indeed for all of us. We found it almost impossible to adapt to it. In no time the inside as well as the outside became a dump, always dirty and unkempt. Inside, there were old rags, horse-hair, feathers and so on, stacked up in every corner of the house. It was the only place where we could keep things dry and safe. Outside we had old scrap strewn all over the place. In all, the house looked a shambles.

This, naturally, brought complaints from our neighbours, and caused many arguments. My younger brothers and sisters were always being jeered by the neighbours' children. When they started school, they were jeered even more. This resulted in their being absent from school a great deal. Worst of all, however, they were hardly able to learn anything, and so they were made to feel very inferior.

My mother took the full brunt of all this. My father could go out and have a few drinks to ease his mind. She, on the other hand, had to stay in the house. When the children came in from school my mother would often ask them how they had got on. As often as not, they would say they had got on well. They did this so that she wouldn't worry. But my mother did worry, both day and night. She knew that the children were getting it very hard at school, and she knew how cruel settled children can be towards children on the road.

In the midst of this I too was beginning to wish we could get away from all this confined living. I was longing to be on the road again, or at least to move away from Mullatty and its atmosphere.

No sooner said than done. This time I didn't need a tent or a wagon; instead the hedgerows, barns and spikes became my resting-places. Within a few days of my starting on the road again, I met and joined company with Joshua, a man of thirty years or so. His long hair and features gave him his nickname. Together we were to travel round Ireland for the best part of a year.

I met Joshua in the 'Mug and Four' café in Townsend Street in Dublin. This café was the haunt of the down-at-heel lot in Dublin. It was an especially hospitable place for those coming out of Mountjoy with nowhere to go. Here they could get a rough-and-ready breakfast for the few shillings they got from the prison authorities. Joshua had just left Mountjoy, where he had done a month for begging in O'Connell Street, a plight that must have turned poor 'Dan' in his grave.

'Hello, there,' he said by way of introduction, 'your face is new round here. What's the matter? Did your ould fella throw you out?'

'In a way,' I said, 'but mostly it was my own wish. I want to try and get a job and settle down.'

'Don't make me laugh,' said Joshua, 'a fat chance you have of getting a job in this God-forsaken city. Some of them here wouldn't give you the blessed Ashes, let alone a job. Job how are you! Do you know what I got for trying to beg the price of a meal? A month! A month's hard labour in the Joy – not that I'm worried – anyway, it was getting a bit cold for the skippers.'

'You mean,' I asked in disbelief, 'that you were in prison? It must be terrible to be in there. I hear they beat you up and everything.'

'Ah no,' said Joshua, 'the Joy is all right, but only for a short time, mind you. It wouldn't do to stay there too long. But in very bad weather it can be as good as the Gresham. Everything's laid on for you – even the grub is good. But that's enough about me, what about you now, where on earth do you hail from?'

'I come from Dara,' I said, 'but most of my life was spent on the road.'

'Oh you're a man after my own heart, a toby-waller. Well I'll say this much, you've picked the right time for the road. With the spring on the doorstep you couldn't go wrong.'

'Are you a pavvy then?' I asked.

'Of course I am, only most of the time I travel alone. I don't know where my parents are, or even if I have any. Most of my life I've had to fend for myself. Mind you, I'm not complaining really, for I get a great amount of happiness betimes.'

'I wish I could say the same,' I said. 'For one thing, I don't like the road, and yet I feel chained to it in a mysterious kind of way.'

'True enough,' said Joshua, 'it's what they call travelling fever in the blood. If you are born to it you can never shake it off. Sure isn't it a grand thing anyway?'

'Yes, it would be nice if there wasn't so much hardship, misery, drunkenness, brawling and sheer cruelty,' I replied.

'True again, but this is only seen when you join and live with what I call the herd. You can, however, get over this, if you take to the road alone, where you can choose your own companions like me. This way you can enjoy road life.'

'Oh, I don't know,' I said, 'I've tried travelling alone before, but things were just as bad.'

'Well,' said Joshua, 'you travel with me for a bit and maybe you will find the road different. Or do you want to stay here in this hell of a city and end up with the winos and meths drinkers? Believe me, this is exactly what will happen if you do. For the likes of you and me, Dublin's only a place of disillusionment.'

'Did you try to get a job here, then?' I asked.

'I tried many things in Dublin and all were an utter failure,' said Joshua. 'Dublin is a place that can turn a man bad. Here fellows like you and me become lazy of life. There is no shortage of a meal or a bed each day. You have the Black Lane, The Morning Star, The Iveagh, the Sally Anne (Salvation Army Hostel) and the workhouse. All of those places break your spirit if you frequent them in your youth. So whatever you do try to keep out of them, otherwise they will grow on you. When that happens you are done for.'

'Well, I'd only stay at those places until I'd got a job and then I would leave,' I said.

'That's what they all say,' said Joshua. 'That's what fellows like Gannet, Charlie the Barber, Dandelion, Seldom Fed and a good many more said and thought when they were young and foolish like you; but all they got was a hell on earth.'

'Gannet,' said I, 'that's a funny name for a person.'

'Yes,' said Joshua, 'but Gannet was not a funny person. He got his name from the way he used to scavenge dustbins to pick up scraps and eat them. It was through meths that he died a violent death at the age of forty. He was drinking the stuff one night when some of it spilled on his clothes. He lit a match to redden a pipe, his clothes caught fire and he was burnt to a cinder in the process.

'Dandelion was a similar character who used to carry around a bunch of dandelion leaves with him, at which he nibbled continuously. He walked under a bus in O'Connell Street and was killed.

'Seldom Fed was found dead from exposure in cold weather; he got his name because he was thin as a rake. As for Charlie the Barber, he cut his throat with the instrument he plied his trade with.'

'That's horrible,' I said. 'It doesn't seem believable.'

'Yes, it is hard to believe, but so is living for the down-and-out in a city. Boy, why should you or I care, we will soon be out of it – at least I will, anyway.'

'Oh, I'll come with you,' I said, 'for a while, anyway.'

'Good, then,' said Joshua, 'the sooner we're on the Naas Road the better, as the cars will be plentiful now. Our first stop will be Cashel, with the help of God; there's a good bed in the spike there. By the way, what can you do for a living, besides mooch? Can you chant or play a box? I mean chant the helms. I'm not a bad chanter meself and if you could play the box or anything we could make a good living.'

'I can't do either,' I replied, 'but I could knob whilst you chant.'

'Yes, sure any old fool can do that, but, however, you'll have to be my knobber,' sighed Joshua.

Off on the road I went with my new-found companion. I liked Joshua for the way he looked at life and I knew that to travel with him for a while might be worth the experience. Joshua, too, to my delight, was a great talker who knew a lot about life; he was funny too, in his ways. And so, as the pair of us high-stepped it off down the Naas Road, I began my questions.

'How long have you been on the road, Joshua?' I asked.

'Oh, since I was knee-high to a duck's eye.'

'Do you really like it, the road I mean?' I asked.

'Oh, most of the time I do but, as I told you, I like to travel alone. I hate following the herd. You see, when I walk along the road alone on a spring day like this I feel happy and contented. Not for me the cares, the grousing, the fighting and the hypocrisy of the herd.'

'Do you believe in your religion, I mean really believe?' I asked.

'Of course I believe in it but I don't always go to Mass or Confession or such-like. Mind, I am not saying it's wrong to go to Mass and that, but again this is part and parcel of the herd instinct which, more often than not, is followed out of sheer hypocrisy.'

'How do you mean?' I asked.

'I mean,' said Joshua, 'that Sunday Mass, for most people, is a hypocritical charade that gives people the idea that they have done something good in the eyes of God.'

'But God said "Blessed is the house in which a crowd is gathered in my name",' I said.

'True, Sean,' said Joshua, 'but when I see the peacocks strutting up and down the aisles of our churches every Sunday morning in their finery, I see it, not as worship of God, but as a fashion show to feed their vanity. Let a poor little tinker-child sit or kneel near one of these peacocks and you will see what I mean.'

'I suppose in a way you're right,' I said, 'but not everyone is like that.'

'True again,' replied Joshua, 'not all are like that and I may be completely wrong, but deep in my heart I feel that I am right. I feel that I can better talk and love my Maker walking along the road. You see, or you probably know, that even Jesus liked to go away and pray alone. He did, as we are told, the greater part of his praying alone.'

'It's funny you should say that,' I interrupted, 'I feel like that too. I always feel better when I pray alone. I get uneasy praying at Mass where there is a crowd of people. It seems to me like being in a pub, at a fair, or the pictures, where all you can hear is a continuous murmuring. When I am alone on the open road talking to God I always feel happy, because then I can forget everything – but I suppose you must think I'm daft for saying this.'

'No, Sean,' said Joshua. 'Not at all; far from it. I pray alone as you do and also enjoy it, a million times better than I would if I were praying in a crowded church.'

'But there is one thing,' I said, 'I keep getting the feeling that when I grow up I will forget all about this. I don't think I would like it if I couldn't have this sort of feeling now and again.'

'I shouldn't worry too much about that,' said Joshua. 'We all have doubts now and again. I very often have very grave doubts about life, but somehow, when I have my little talk with God without anyone to distract my thoughts, I can feel happy again.'

'You know,' I said 'you're funny; I mean the way you talk about things.'

'Ah musha, it's a funny world we live in, son! All the likes of yourself and meself on the road can do is to step out in the morning and beg our biteen of food and search for a decent mollying ground to pitch a tent. For those with a large family to rear on the road, life becomes that much harder to bear.'

'I often think about this,' I said, 'and when I do it doesn't seem right. I feel angry too with the travelling parents; why don't they try to better their ways? All they seem to want to do is drink all the time.'

'Son,' said Joshua, 'this is a fact of road life, one of the cruellest and most primitive ways of existence. Through its many phases of loneliness and hardship, families, for generations, have become depressed and oppressed beyond all belief. Drink is an outlet for their fears and unhappiness.

'The gentry – and by that I mean all the settled community – care little for us, just as we care little about them other than to beg all we can from them. The nub of the whole thing is that we are entirely independent of the settled community. They pay us no respect because we are as useless to them as their lowliest animal.'

'Yes,' I said, 'it does seem very wrong. Why can't everyone help and love each other? It would be lovely if everyone did this, then everyone could be friends. You know, when I was a small boy I went to a good many houses to beg and was often invited in to share a dinner or supper with a family; many a time I stayed sitting by a big warm fire for hours chatting with the family. Do you know that I always treasured such happy moments and wished, with all my heart, that it could be like that always?'

'True, Sean,' said Joshua, 'there are many good and kind

people like this who always make you happy and wanted and cared for when you enter their house; but – and this is most important in a Christian country – every house should welcome those less fitted for life than they are, by the grace of God.'

'Why do people not do this?' I asked. 'If I had plenty of money I would help all I could. To me, giving things to other people and making them happy would make me happy. Say, for instance, I have a pal and I go out begging with him; if I begged more than him during the day I would share out what I got so that we both would have the same. Perhaps you will laugh at this but if I didn't do this I couldn't feel really happy.'

'Oh no, Sean,' said Joshua, 'I would not laugh at all, for I'd do the same myself. I will never see a fellow traveller short if I have anything at all to give him. But wealth or good deeds are not what makes for happiness, but friendship and love or being wanted, as when you got your invitations to eat with families. This is what is really needed. If I were to be given thousands of pounds as a handout at a door, I would still feel unwanted. You'd feel the same if the families, instead of inviting you in, had given you the food wrapped up in a bit of paper to be taken away. You would not have felt happy, like you did when you sat at the table!'

'Yes,' I said, 'I see what you mean about having friends.'

'Well,' said Joshua, 'so much for friends; now, the important thing is, can we find someone to give us a lift to Cashel and also somewhere to eat? Here, thumb this car coming now and pray that it will stop.'

The car did stop and Joshua and I were carried even further than Cashel. The driver told us he was going to Cahir, so, it being a good long day, we decided to go all the way there and walk the few miles back to Cashel. We both knew that Cahir was a good town to mooch.

It was still early in the day when we arrived in Cahir; the first thought on our minds when we got there was peck, so off to the nearest convent we went for our meal, for they were our main source for food as we travelled from town to town.

When we got to the convent at Cahir, we met Tommy-the-Stook. He was wiring into a feed of fé and cunnions. When we too had had our share we soon got chatting to him. His name was apt, for most of the time he stood quite still; even when he ate, his hand went to his pei like a robot. Tommy-the-Stook was a man of thirty or so, though he looked more like sixty.

I took an instant liking to him. He told us that he chanted the helms. On hearing this, Joshua became very interested in our new-found friend.

'Well, Tommy,' he asked, 'what way are ye heading, if you don't mind me asking?'

'Oh, I'm goin' to Tipperary town,' replied Tommy. 'That's a great town to chant. You two can come along if you want to do a bit of knobbing for me.'

Joshua and I readily agreed, for we both knew that a good chanter could earn good money on the drags.

After our meal at the convent in Cahir with Tommy-the-Stook, we headed for Tipperary, stopping at the spike in Thurles that night.

'The three of us arrived in Tipperary town the next morning at about 11.00. We found that it was fair day, and pretty packed with people.

Anyway, Tommy-the-Stook gave me an old cap. 'Now,' he said, 'you take one side for the drag and let your friendeen there take the other, and start knobbing when I start singing.'

Joshua and I took up our respective positions on either side of the street, waiting for our balladeer to burst into song. Joshua and I felt sure we were going to make a handy few quid, and an easy few too.

Despite the din of the passing cars, Tommy broke into song. Never in my life had I heard a voice like I did in Tipperary town that morning, and never do I want to hear it again.

At first I couldn't believe my ears, so I looked back at Tommy to make sure; there, true enough, with mouth wide open, he stood giving 'Galway Bay' the biggest murdering it ever got or is ever likely to either.

I glanced from Tommy to Joshua to see if he had noticed from the far side of the street. When I caught sight of him words were not needed; the expression of surprise and fear on his face was enough.

It was the voice that did it. At one pitch, it sounded like a jackass hee-hawing, rising to an ear-splitting screech, like a horse neighing. Tommy was not chanting quietly or softly. He was roaring his head off, and it could be heard from one end of the town to the other.

I had begun to get frightened by now, for I thought that poor Tommy had taken a stroke or something, like the crowing hen or the dog with fits that keeps barking all the time.

Without more ado I ran over to Joshua, who was every bit as shocked as myself.

'Listen, lad,' he said, 'the best thing we can do is crush away lively, because in my opinion, that so-called street singer is a stark-raving madman and we are just as mad to be with him.'

Meanwhile Tommy was still bawling wildly and, to make things worse, a large crowd had gathered to hear the singing hyena, and they began throwing money galore on the ground around him.

On seeing this, Joshua grabbed me and said 'Get in there quick feen with that cadie. Look at all that grade pouring in.' So, forgetting all else, Joshua and I started picking the money off the ground.

On seeing this, someone in the crowd shouted, 'That's it lads, pick it up, and then the three of you can sing the "Donkey Serenade" for us. I'd say you'd make a lovely trio.' This caused a good deal of laughter, but the money was still pouring in.

Suddenly the voice stopped singing, and Joshua and I looked around to see what had happened. It was then we. heard a big burly garda shouting, 'Hey, I want you two as well, come along to the station with me. The sergeant would like a word with you lot.'

As the three of us were marched to the garda station,

Joshua turned to me. 'I told you that your man there was a lunatic.'

I didn't answer him, I was so scared. My pockets were bulging with money, as were Joshua's.

'Well, well, what have we here, Tommy?' asked the sergeant, when we got to the station. 'Are they bank robbers or grave robbers?'

'No, Sarge,' replied the garda, 'I would kind of admire them if that were so. That yob there, the funny looking one, was bawling his head off on the street; singing he calls it, singing how are ye! In truth, Sarge, I thought he was some lunatic who had escaped. However,' he continued, 'I gave him a bit of advice and told him he should give up singing for a living, at least until he got some voice training.'

On hearing this Joshua and I burst out laughing. 'Here now,' roared the sergeant, 'get out of this barracks as quick as your legs can carry you, the whole three of you. Laughing!' he bellowed, 'I'll give you laughing if I ever catch you around these parts again.'

When we got outside the town, we all sat by the roadside and shared out the takings, which were very good. Then Joshua and I parted company with Tommy-the-Stook. I shall always remember Tommy-the-Stook as being a very comical character. Ironically, he still maintains that he is a good singer.

'We'll head back for Cashel, Sean,' said Joshua, 'I've had enough of the Stook, he'd only get us arrested.'

'Okay, Josh,' I said, 'maybe it's as well.'

So we headed for Cashel, Joshua and I. Joshua was, as I said before, a strange and likeable character and I began to copy him in a way. During the time I was with him so far, I had learned a great deal. I had been to many places with him and his ways were becoming my ways. I, too, was becoming cynical about life. Joshua had a chip on his shoulder against society, and because I was so fond of him I too was getting a kind of chip of my own.

Joshua was a man who could argue and argue. On our travels, he would argue with me about life in general; all the time he was drawing me out. Strangely enough, we were in two different worlds with regard to experience of life; Joshua was a veteran while I was an amateur, but he was quickly making me catch up with him.

'How long were you put away for?' said Joshua, trying me out.

'I wasn't *put* away, I *went*,' I replied.

'Well, how long were you away?'

'Four years.'

'Yeh must have learned a power of things, then,' said Joshua with some respect. 'I dunno though, I don't think I'd like it with the Brothers floggin' you round the place all the time.'

'Were you there?'

'No, but I heard all about it.'

'Well you heard wrong; I never saw anyone flogged around in Joseph's. And I saw a lot of slags that could have done with it.'

A dozen faces from the school flashed across my mind, lads who had defied the Brothers' best efforts to educate them.

'It wasn't a bad place,' I said. 'Not a bad place at all. You'd get browned-off at times when nothing was happening, and there were often times when you'd like to walk off down the drive and not come back, but something always turned up to break the monotony. Like the time....'

'Wasn't it all rules and orders?' Joshua suggested.

'No more than at home,' I said.

'But weren't they always trying to climb up on your back, for no reason at all?'

'Aren't pavvies well used to that? Isn't somebody always after the travellers – the law or the welfare....'

'Or the Legion,' said Joshua.

'They have no cop-on. They make rules and regulations to suit themselves,' I said, 'anything that will make things hard for the poor.'

'Come off it,' said Joshua. 'Now you're havin' me on. I thought I was the one with the grouse against the settled people. You're worse than me.'

'I'm not, then. We were camped one night in the rain on the side of a bad road, the grub-box was empty and the da had drunk the Home Assistance. I remember a car stopping and a man getting out. Before he could speak, my mother asked him for a little help. He turned and went back to the car and arrived back immediately with a census form. By God, that's one form that never got filled.'

11

We had a hearty meal at the convent, and then to while away a bit of time before going to the County Home for the night, we went to see the Rock of Cashel. Standing there, I could almost hear the monks chanting, and the sound of the bells in the background. It was a strange feeling. But Joshua was not impressed.

'Oh, look down at the bottom of the hill, Sean,' he said suddenly, 'there are some pavvies down there.'

'Yes, we camped there years ago. It's a good mollying ground. I wonder who they are. I can only see one wagon, but there might be tents there as well. It won't ate us to go down and see who are there, it could be someone we know.'

'We might stay with them for a night? It'll be a change anyway and we can spike it here some other time, God spare us.'

We forgot the splendour of the 'Rock' and went straight down to the travellers' molly. As it turned out we knew them. It was the Rinnacuddy family.

'Well, well,' said Joshua, as we reached the camp, 'if it isn't ould Chew-the-Cud himself, how are you all these days? Still chanting the helms?'

'I declare to God!' said ould Jim. 'Look, Nelly girl, look who's dropped in, holy Moses himself and his new disciple, Mickeen Devine's son, Sean. Come and sit down the pair of you and we'll have a talk over a bit of peck. Where are you staying anyway? Near here?'

'Well, to tell you the truth,' said Joshua, 'we're tobying it alone these days.'

'Spikes is it? Well that's good,' said Jim, 'you can kip with my lads. I hope you'll stay a few days. The lads will be delighted to meet the pair of you.'

'How many have you now?' asked Joshua, 'or have you given up tumbling in the strumble with the missus?'

'The divil a give up,' said Jim, 'I'll still enjoy my tumble. At any rate we have twelve children but they're all away from us now, all married except the three young lads, Philip, Felix and Francis – the three fools I call them. Francis is the youngest – he's twelve; then there's Felix who's fourteen, and Philip is sixteen. They went to the chats not long ago.'

'How's Nelly?'

'Cranky as ever. All she ever thinks about is grade.'

'By the look of your gills, she's looking after you,' said Joshua.

A short while later the three lads got back from the pictures.

'Well, here they are,' said Jim, 'my three fools; Gomey, alias Philip; Bless you, alias Felix, and Chew-the-Cud junior, alias Francis, or Chewy as we call him now.'

'Well, it's nice to see you lads again,' said Joshua. 'By the way, Gomey, do you still give out over your nickname?'

'Give out be damned!' interrupted Jim, 'it rolls off him like water off a duck's back. At times that big fool of mine is a real gomey. Only the other day, another pavvy, ould Rogs Eye Sweeney, of all people, gave the gomey here an old mangy comeragh and told him to carry it in his arms to the police station and ask for a free dog licence. And would you believe that the fool here took the mangy dog in his arms to the barracks and did ask the garda for a free licence off him?'

'If you only knew the trouble I had in getting him out of the barracks that day.'

'Arrah, I wouldn't take much notice of that,' said Joshua, laughing, 'you have three fine lads. They must be great company.'

'Sure I'm always saying this,' said Nelly. 'Don't you pair miss home? I don't think that Sean there is very wise to be going around as he is – and you're worse, Joshua, for encouraging him.'

'Here, now, Nelly, don't be blaming me. He was going it alone when I met him. I thought that a bit of company would be good for him.'

'Company my eye!' said Nelly. 'He has all the company he needs at home with his family, and much better company too.'

'Ah, it's not that, missus,' I said, 'you can't blame Joshua. It's entirely my own choosing. You see my parents have settled in a house. I was with them for the first year or so, but somehow the urge hit me.'

'You belong with your parents, not roaming around the tramps' heartbreaks,' said Nelly.

'To hell with my parents,' said I without thinking.

'Shame on you,' said Nelly. 'You....'

'That's what education does for you,' interrupted Jim. 'They're not good enough for you any more. I always said education's of no use to travelling people. None of mine have had it and they're the better for it.'

'They are like hell,' said I. 'Look at them, three fine lads. And what can they expect outa life living in a filthy, smelly little tent on the side of a road, pickin' over other people's rubbish for a living or beggin' like cripples in the street. If being away at school taught me that there's more in life than that, then I'm glad I was at school.'

'Road life has done us no harm,' said Jim, 'nor my parents, or even your own good mother and father.'

'You're only coddin' yourself now, Jim,' said I. And I thought of my father trying to drink himself out of his misery and into a better, if imaginary, life. I thought of nights listening to the wheeze in my brother's chest and his gasps after the damp smoky air of the tent. I thought of bright lights in small windows with lace curtains and the smell of new bread as I passed the door. But what was the use. It was no good talking to Chew-the-Cud and maybe I'd be doing more harm than good if I made him less happy with his lot. 'Every man to his taste,' said I, and left it at that.

But Jim was no fool.

'Say what yer thinkin,' he said, 'like a man.'

His words hurt. It was then I realised that if I had a message I would have to become a missioner. If I learned something Jim and his family didn't know, it was my duty to tell them.

'You're all thinkin' that it was Mickeen Devine's buckled belt that made me a loner,' I began. 'You said yourself it was my bit of schoolin'. Yet you know in your heart that every man, sooner or later, gets curious about everything, big or small, that affects his life.

'You know there are times when I say to myself, oh to hell with religion, to hell with settled life, what's wrong with the road? Then again I think... well, why shouldn't I care? You can't really say it's education or anything like that makes me think like this, but rather the mystery of life itself. With each day that passes, this world becomes more valueless for me. No, education has not altered me, it has only made me more aware of the falsity of life around me. Maybe it wouldn't be a bad idea to travel the roads alone. Getting away from humanity for a time might clear my head and calm my mind.'

'That's the way, me lad,' said Joshua, 'now you're talking sense. Go it alone and forget about jobs or work, just mooch and mooch, and to hell with everyone. No one cares for us, so we'll care less for them. Tomorrow, Sean, we'll head for Cork and then on to Kerry and we won't stop this side of Killorglin.'

'I'm sorry, Joshua,' I said, 'but, much as I like you, I won't be able to travel with you for very long. I know that the two of us together would get on all right as long as we'd care to stay together; but, though we'd have a few laughs on the way, I'd still feel the need to be alone. It's just that I'm tired of the whole mess of my mixed-up way of living and I think that this is the only way I can clear my thoughts.'

'That's the kind of silly statement we all make when we're young,' said Joshua. 'All too often we live to regret them. But no matter what we say, Jim, it won't make any difference; we can only hope that he will correct his ideas as they seem to go wrong, and besides, he may yet change his mind. There's nothing like a bit of hardship for curing one's ambitions.'

'Well, it hasn't cured you,' said Jim, 'so you can't really talk. The best thing Sean can do, as I have said, is forget all this hermit trash and go back to his family.'

'I won't listen to any more of this,' I said, 'if you go on any longer I'll leave right away.'

'Oh, all right, Sean,' said Joshua, 'tomorrow is another day.'

'Yes,' I murmured, 'only God knows what a new day has in store for us; only he really knows what the future holds for each and every one of us. But what I see – if seeing it is – is something very bleak, something that drives me to search, and search very deeply, for a way of escape.'

'What on earth are you mumbling about now?' asked Jim. 'You and your thoughts; you *are* too deep, if you ask me.'

'I wish people wouldn't keep saying this,' I said, 'Why is it that, no matter what I say, people think it strange?'

'Well, it's the way you talk about things, Sean,' explained Jim. 'People – like myself for instance – look at a bit of stick as part of a living tree, which is really of no importance.'

'But it *is* important,' I said, 'to me, anyway; all life is important, otherwise what need is there for me – or you for that matter – on the earth? There must be a reason and a plan for everything, and it's because I try to understand this that my thoughts are always turning. For me it is a compulsion; why, I don't know.'

'Now, if I were you, lad, I'd forget all this nonsense,' said Nelly, 'after all, the road has done little harm to us, or to your own parents for that matter.'

'What is ever any good on the road?' I asked. 'In all our begging, swapping and dealing what can we show for it? Nothing; nothing but loneliness, misery and an unending unhappiness; that continues till our premature deaths. This is not life; this is not a fit existence for even a dog, let alone a human being.

'So you can understand why,' I continued, 'for the past twelve years or more most of my thoughts have been about the road and the people who have wandered it through the centuries. I have listened to thousands of tales about them and been completely enraptured by them. When I began school, particularly when listening to the history lessons, I was taken back to the road in past centuries. Although I was hearing the written history of Ireland for the first time, somehow I had heard it all before, only that it concerned the travellers and not the so-called great soldiers and kings. It was the same with the Irish language of the Irish people and had been so for centuries. I remember how I used to argue with the teachers about this. I used to tell them that they were forgetting "Cant" – the traveller's language. They often told me that this is only associated with ignorant people.

'Remembering, too, the many great old storytellers I have known and listened to on the road as a boy, I can easily overlook the truth of the official written history of Ireland.

'Whatever else one can say about the travellers of Ireland it can't be said that they are inclined towards exaggeration or lying.'

'Yes,' said Joshua, 'I'll grant you that, but, just the same, a lot of the tales are of the superstitious kind.'

'Oh, yes,' I said, 'we have a lot of superstitions. But you must remember too that all of these have come down from early Christian times unchanged and, for the most part, unheard of by so-called society.'

'Yes, but I bet you don't know all the superstitions the travellers have,' interrupted Joshua.

'Well I think I do,' I said, 'at least I know the unique and unusual ones.'

'What unusual ones?' asked Joshua.

'Well, how many of you here at this fire like jam?' I asked.

'I don't eat jam,' said Joshua.

'We don't eat it either,' Jim said. 'None of us do because it brings bad luck,'

'Oh,' I said, 'does anyone know why?'

'No,' said Jim and Joshua, almost together.

'Well, it began (and I thought of old Hannora Bell

telling it at a fire one night, back in Clare) during the last famine. The people were dying all over the country and the travellers, as you can imagine, were in a worse plight, for they were dependent on the settled people for their food. Since the people's main source of food, their crops of potatoes, had failed, things looked bleak indeed for the travellers. At first, the travellers did not even know about the failure of the crops. They went around the country begging, but in vain; they were given nothing, for there was nothing to give; then the travellers noticed that a lot of people in the houses and farms were dying; but they just assumed that the people had fallen on evil times because of their meanness.

'Anyway,' I continued, 'the travellers had to turn to eating herbs, berries, roots and any other edible things they could find along the hedgerows. They even resorted to killing and eating their own goats – almost sacred animals to them – in order to satisfy their hunger. Then supplies slowly began coming into Ireland, and with them loads of fruit. It was this that started things off.

'Someone – in a well-meaning and generous way – began boiling the fruit in large metal pots, making a kind of jam. When this was made it was given out here and there to the starving people of Ireland. The fruit was cooked to keep it from getting bad. It was a kind of preserve. Travellers had got together, united in their worry about the way they were being hunted away from everyone's door. They didn't know that there was a famine in the country; indeed, even when they heard the word they didn't know what it meant; they thought it was just an excuse for the people to refuse to give them anything.

'Well, to make a long story short,' I continued, 'some women carrying a large cauldron on an old cart came to an encampment of travellers one day, and started dishing out this boiled fruit concoction to all the travellers, who ate it greedily. However, within a week of their eating this boiled fruit, death had taken its toll, mostly among the children. All of them had suffered severe stomach pains. The fruit caused most of the deaths in the encampment, mainly because these people had eaten no kind of substantial food for months, other than what they picked from the hedgerows. However, the travellers who survived the ordeal blamed only those who had given them the boiled fruit; they were convinced that they had been given poison, and nothing ever will convince them otherwise; as you know, to this day they will not eat jam.'

'I heard something about this years ago too,' said Jim, 'but I always heard the jam was a witch's food.'

'Do you know the one about the greyhounds and the hare?' asked Joshua.

'If a greyhound keens on a moonlit night it means death to the head of the family or families who hear it,' said I. 'If a hare cries (and when it does, it's like a baby's cry) it means death to the youngest of the family who hears it.

'There are many more superstitions peculiar to travellers, magpies, for instance, or a dog that cake-walks – or their abhorrence of frogs.

'The one about the hare began on a spring day many years ago when twenty or so travelling men went hunting with about six greyhounds. They brought with them two young children, two little boys of about five or six. They were both the youngest children of large families.

'Anyway, when the men were ferreting out some rabbit burrows, the two children strayed over the fields with the six greyhounds. While they were with them the hounds ousted a hare and caught it.

'The men heard the screams of a dying hare – they easily recognised this, having hunted them so often. But they couldn't see the dogs, or where the hare had been attacked, so they continued their ferreting. About ten or twenty minutes later they heard more screams; this time, however, they were not those of a hare – this much they did know.

'Without a second's delay all of the men ran in the direction from where the screams had come. After climbing through a few hedges they came upon a sight that made them stop in their tracks in sheer horror, for there, lying in torn pieces, were the bloodied remains of the two children, entangled with those of the hare. The dogs were chasing each other unconcernedly around the field.

'The men picked up the bodies of the children and took them back to the camp. For over a week afterwards there was great lamenting and hundreds of travellers came from miles around to the wake. After this the children were buried by the roadside and the family left the spot.

'The strange thing is that the families blamed the hare for killing the children; they found out that the hare had been in young when the dogs killed it and believed that she had taken her revenge on them. They never accused the real culprits, which were, of course, the greyhounds. I suppose that when the hounds killed the hare the children got in their midst to take the hare from them, and the dogs duly turned on the children and mauled them to death, However, it is traditionally believed to have been the work of the hare or some evil associated with her.

'The same can be said about the belief in the banshee. The original banshee was a travelling woman and her story is a tragic one:

'A very long time ago there was a man and his wife and six children, who were camping by the roadside in the heart of Kerry. The wife had spent the day begging through the countryside while her husband stopped at the camp minding the children. Anyway, on this particular day the wife was very late getting home for she had walked a great distance that day.

'However, when she got back to the camp, around about midnight, she found the camp completely burned to the ground, and with it her husband and six children. All that was left was their charred remains.

'I needn't tell you that the woman completely lost her mind, and for days, and even months after, she could be heard going around the roads keening in a most eerie way. Most people took little notice of her, she being a travelling woman, and it wasn't unusual to hear them crying or roaring about some domestic quarrel. Around the place where the tragedy occurred she could be heard very plainly, particularly at night when everything was quiet.

'Then people began to notice this woman, who was always described as the most wretched-looking person they ever saw. She was ragged and dirty, and as she keened she seemed to be pulling lumps out of her matted, greying hair.

'This went on for months, until one day the dead body of this heartbroken mother was found lying by the roadside, her body half-eaten by rats. No one knew who she was, or of the great sorrow she had gone through. But around that part of the country the people say that the woman's keening can still be heard at night. Over the years the story of the keening woman became more widespread until eventually she became known as the "banshee".

'So, even to this day the banshee is still believed in. And many superstitions like this have come down through the ages, told and retold by the travelling people themselves. Sorrow or tragedy endured by travellers is never forgotten, no matter how many years go by.'

'But there is such a thing as a banshee,' said Jim's wife.

'Sure she was seen and heard too not long ago when the Kinly's child died. Mrs Kinly herself saw her.'

'I'm not doubting for one minute that there is such a thing as a banshee,' I answered, 'but what I am saying is that among the travellers anyway the banshee is never seen or heard until someone dies in a family, and even then is only seen by people with certain names, such as that of the original woman who lost her family all those years ago.'

12

The talk went on and at last we settled down for the night and I lay there deciding that I must walk my road alone. So, when all were asleep, I got up and quietly left the camp, then sauntered down the road to meet my destiny. As I walked the long moonlit road, my thoughts were very active. 'I've done it again,' I thought. 'I've made my choice; good or bad, I have made it. They were good friends I sneaked out on back there.'

'That's me all over,' I thought, 'I am good for making decisions, but how good? As I walk this road now, let me examine the milestones of the many roads of the past. Road,' I thought. 'That word haunts me.' Well, the road was my home and cradle, as it was for my ancestors. I know it has a great and ancient history, passed down by the word of mouth true and faithfully, completely unknown to the buffer, and lost or ignored in the annals of Irish history.

Behind me, too, is the culture and folklore of the travelling people, probably unique in the world, a people who stand still as the rest of civilisation races on. To what?

Yet, within myself, I am a bit happier now that I am voicing these thoughts on this lonely ramble. In a way it eases my mind and in a way I am thankful. I fear tomorrow, the unknown, the great and everlasting tomorrow. What of that?

What of my parents who are learning to settle? What of the many poor wanderers of the road? Are they now, in this age, condemned to wander aimlessly? Will pity, love and understanding turn the blind eye on them for ever?

Now I trundle along this earthly road and, once again, I am forsaking my parents and friends, once again I search for reason, sanity and, most of all, happiness. Whether I shall experience such in this world, I know not; but I shall try, come what may.

Oh, here I go again, reading my own thoughts. It's amazing how they pass through one's mind. The great thing about thought is that it can give one great personal elation betimes. Even now, on this heavenly dawning day, as I tread onwards, my thoughts are beautifully distracted by the sound of God's feathered creatures bursting into morning song. How I envy the birds' joyous song; for them, sweet creatures, song is contentment, joy and happiness.

Thus, carried away by my thoughts and the wonder of nature, I walk easily down the winding road; the morning light just creeping in, the birdsong beginning to burst into a symphony of beautiful sound. Listening and drunk with rapture, a tear and a smile come together, for I feel good at this break of a new day, heralded by a million voices of God's feathered creatures. Times like this are heaven to me, taking me into a different and more beautiful world.

It is fitting then to enjoy this great enchantment of the new day, for days like these are precious. This one is especially so, for with it begins a new journey and only God knows what lies ahead. The future holds fear for all of us. Each person journeys a lonely road, and, as is the way of all roads, they hold many hidden obstacles. No road is trouble-free, but with the aid of a spiritual radar can be less treacherous or shameful. As with all journeys, the start is always the most pleasant, but as you travel further and further, the more tiresome it becomes. For such as us on the road, the journey can be a nightmare, for it's often a journey of darkness, where one is ever probing to find the switch to light up some of the way.

I found, maybe, one such switch, which gave me a splash of light for four short years; it was the kindling of education. It was, however, a kindling that sparked off an unquenchable thirst to learn more about my people who have journeyed so long through the centuries. Even in the pale light, as I come to a little crossroads, I can see where a travelling family have taken the road to the right, by simply looking at some tufts of grass strewn on the road, simple signs that are ancient and unique, without a shred of meaning to any but the travelling people. I look at these tufts of grass, strewn into an arc, about a foot apart.

I can even see, by the coloration of the grass, that they were travelling late last night and that whoever was following had not done so yet, because if they had, they would have removed the tufts of grass from the road, thereby avoiding confusion for other travellers who pass along the way.

Looking at this simple sign once again makes my heart heavy, for it recalls the times I followed and found my own parents with tufts of grass. I remember how I used to examine the tuft of grass to make sure that it was my parents' grass and not that of some other travelling family. I remember how my parents told me, when I was quite young, always to put one piece of twig from a bush with each tuft of grass. That way, they said, anyone of our family and close relations would know that it was one of us who strewed the grass at the crossroads and not another family. Our grass marks were always made in this way.

Each and every family had their own way of making this simple sign of direction. Some went by the number of tufts they put down, others by the distance between each tuft or by putting a small stone with each tuft. But most important of all was that the person following always had to clear the grass from the road when they got to a crossroads.

As I journeyed along on this morning, these signs carried away my thoughts with their sheer simplicity. I knew in my heart that soon this simplicity would be no more, that a people, a language and a culture would die in this horrible, modern world. On seeing this simplicity, I loved and hated the road, for different reasons.

As I reach the first brow of a hill on this road, the morning is well risen. I take a look back along the road I have come, and I can see a kind of gentle people, my people, soon to be contaminated by the horribleness of modern ethics and thinking, a grave insult to God, the Creator of all.

I know not what lies on the far side of the hill but I know I must waddle forward, like a duck, unsure of my footing.

Life is like this, we all waddle through the short span of life. In reality, each and every one of us is on the road, and one day, please God, we shall all meet at the final mollying ground; then the road shall end, and for some it will be a very happy molly. There too we will, by the grace of God, meet the Saviour who travelled and mollied in his humble earthly life. With such thoughts life has meaning, and with meaning I can journey with the rest of humanity on the road that leads to God knows where.

Phrases and Sayings

Travelling people may often be understood only amongst themselves. Words are pronounced as in Gaelic, thus indicating the origin of this almost extinct language. Here are a few common phrases:

Salc the srothar and srúti the rodus.
Take the key and shut the door.

Scóp the rodus (jigger).
Open the door.

Lush your grichéir.
Eat your dinner.

Do you grane tómán garéid?
Do you want much money?

The Tásp may lúb you.
Back luck to you.

The beor of the cean bucéads the ríspa.
The woman of the house wears the trousers.

Láisiúil tálosc.
Fine day.

Mílse is corrib'd with the goop.
I am perished with the cold.

Crádi your pei!
Shut your mouth!

Géig a lush from the beor.
Ask a drink for the woman.

A ruspan of garéad.
A purse of money.

Stagish the laceen tori'n arais the tober.
Look at the girl coming back the road.

Inoc gaiste of the steamer.
Smoke plenty of the pipe.

I'll gréti my luighe in this lúrcán.
I'll make my bed in this corner.

Buri tálosc to your jeel.
Good luck to you.

Searcin' stáin.
Cutting tin.

Stéis.
I am.

Ní déis.
I am not.

Tabhraigh nailc of eyaid for the durra.
Give (me) a bit of butter for the bread.

He could not lush the roomógs without the salan.
He could not eat the eggs without salt.

Misligh into the luighe, it is getting dorchóg!

Hurry to bed, it is getting dark (night)!

Glossary of Cant or Shelta words

Aisht . . . . .listen
Alamuck . . . . .milk
Anosha . . . . .immediately
Beor . . . . .travelling woman
Buffer . . . . .settled person
Busker . . . . .street musician
Cadie . . . . .cap
Cant . . . . .talk
Carnish . . . . .unsalted meat
Cean . . . . .house
Ceania . . . . .big house
Chanter . . . . .singer
Chats . . . . .things
Choicer . . . . .nothing
Chuck . . . . .food
Clem . . . . .spoil
Coller . . . . .take
Comeragh . . . . .dog
Comóg . . . . .pup
Conger . . . . .cake, bread
Conie . . . . .rabbit
Conie tug . . . . .rabbit-skin
Conish . . . . .frightened
Connia . . . . .dirt
Cories . . . . .feet
Corrip . . . . .beat
Crabs . . . . .boots
Creeper . . . . .cat
Croak . . . . .die
Crolish . . . . .hungry

Cronies . . . . .favourites
Crush . . . . .go
Cúnia . . . . .priest
Cunic . . . . .monk
Cunnions . . . . .potatoes
Curra . . . . .horse
Deener . . . . .English shilling
Diffles . . . . .fiddles
Donar . . . . .street
Dreeper . . . . .bottle
Drubbers . . . . .sticks
Durra . . . . .loaf or leaven bread
Durriger . . . . .fortune-teller
Eyaid . . . . .butter
Fé . . . . .salted meat
Feen . . . . .travelling man
Fógaré . . . . .cigar
Fountie . . . . .tap water
Gaigue . . . . .beg
Gallia . . . . .child
Gallúme . . . . .goodness
Gammon . . . . .cant
Gammy . . . . .bad
Gat . . . . .porter
Gat-cean . . . . .public-house
Gills . . . . .face
Gimurs . . . . .shoes
Glazer . . . . .window
Gleib . . . . .hair
Glim . . . . .light
Glimmer . . . . .fire
Gloke . . . . .look
Gom . . . . .foolish
Gomóg . . . . .young fool
Grade . . . . .money
Grade-sac . . . . .money-pocket
Grunter . . . . .pig
Helm . . . . .town

Innic . . . . .item or thing
Jigger . . . . .door
Joes . . . . .Protestants
Jonnic . . . . .watch
Knobbing . . . . .collecting
Laceen . . . . .girl
Laiteóg . . . . .lady
Larc . . . . .cart
Larry . . . . .hump
Lee, luighe . . . . .bed
Lunter . . . . .Irish pound
Lush . . . . .drink
Main, Monicer . . . . .name
Malias . . . . .hands
Mallard . . . . .donkey
Mealtug . . . . .trousers
Merdie . . . . .cycle
Mideog . . . . .Irish shilling
Missle . . . . .move
Molly . . . . .camp
Molly-iron . . . . .kettle bar
Monia . . . . .happy day
Mooch . . . . .beg
Mungie . . . . .food sack
Nopper, Niuc . . . . .head
Nork . . . . .steal
Nump . . . . .English pound
Ogans . . . . .marks
Oglers . . . . .eyes
Onsha . . . . .alone
Pad . . . . .trade
Padder . . . . .trader
palem . . . . .Communion bread
Pavvy . . . . .traveller
Peck . . . . .food
Pei . . . . .mouth
Pragg, Prague . . . . .heavy horse
Rack . . . . .comb

Reader ....ballad sheet
Rog ....motor
Roomógs ....hen eggs
Roots ....new potatoes
Rouler ....cart
Router ....goat milk
Ruilla ....mad
Salan ....salt
Salery ....cabbage
Sark ....field
Scuie ....river water
Scutchy ....matted
Shadeog, Shade ....Garda
Sham ....settled man
Shelta-Molly ....talking tent
Spike ....county home
Staish ....hold on
Stall ....stop
Steamers ....cigarettes
Stir ....jail
Strumble ....straw-bed
Sublia ....lad
Swag ....things for sale
Sweetie, Rugar ....sugar
Tacklers ....goose eggs
Tober ....road
Toie ....night
Torrig ....see
Trimmers ....sticks
Traipe ....alcoholic drink
Tugs ....clothes
Waxie ....lino
Weed ....tea
Whid ....talk
Wide ....in the know
Wob ....soldier